Mariachiara Pozzana

GARDENS
of FLORENCE
and TUSCANY

A COMPLETE GUIDE

GIUNTI

Project and editorial coordination:
Camilla Giunti

Graphics:
Giovanni Breschi

Text revision and page format:
Guillaume Tietzte

Translation:
Catherine Frost

Drawings:
Drawings of the gardens by Cristina Basaldella
for the studio *Architettura e Paesaggio*
by Mariachiara Pozzana.

Maps:
Legenda, Novara

Photographs:
Nicola Grifoni, Florence (p. 13); Fondazione
Collodi (p. 109); Alessandro Tombelli, Florence
(pp. 83, 160, 161d, 168, 181);
Archivio Giunti, Florence (pp. 16, 59, 93);
Unless otherwise indicated, the photographs
are taken from the Archivio Giovanni Breschi,
Florence.

Acknowledgements:
The author wishes to thank all those who have
collaborated in the realization of this book as
well as the owners of villas and gardens who
have made their property available for
photographs and information, in particular:
Livia Aldobrandini Pediconi, Anna Balsamo,
Maria Teresa Benedetti, Ferdinando and
Laura Budini Gattai, Massimo Canizza,
Filippo and Giorgiana Corsini, Vittoria Colonna,
Gil Cohen and Paul Gervais, Giovanna Donato,
Giuliano Gori, Lorenza Stucchi Prinetti,
Luisa Oliva, Francesca Grabau, Anna Marchi,
Carla Mazzei, Paolo Peyron, Paola and Anna
Porcinai, Vanni Pozzolini, Alberto Sandrelli and
Maria Sofia Sandrelli Duranti, Lorenzo Scaretti,
Andrea Scavetta, Daniel Spoerri,
Vieri Torrigiani, Luigi Zalum.

As well as the Bureaus:
Soprintendenza ai Beni Ambientali
Architettonici Artistici e Storici di Pisa,

Soprintendenza ai Beni Ambientali
Architettonici Artistici e Storici di Arezzo,
Soprintendenza ai Beni Ambientali e
Architettonici di Firenze,
Soprintendenza ai Beni Ambientali
e Architettonici di Siena,
Orto Botanico di Firenze,
Associazione Dimore Storiche della Toscana,
Cassa di Risparmio di Pisa,
Fondazione Parchi Monumentali Bardini
e Peyron, promoted by Ente Cassa di
Risparmio di Firenze,
Fondazione Nazionale Carlo Collodi,
Direzione Sezione Ambiente del Comune
di Firenze,
New York University, Villa La Pietra.

A sincere thanks to friends:
Pier Francesco Bernacchi, Sandro Di Mare,
Maria Rita and Enrico Guadagni,
François Roche.

*Thanks also, for their continuous collaboration,
to*: Giuseppe Bagnoli; for invaluable information
on citrus trees Paolo Galeotti;
for the photographic material kindly made
available Alessandro Tombelli;
for having furnished the material
for the following texts: Tessa Matteini
(Orti Oricellari, Giardino Corsi, Villa Caruso,
Giardino Catastini, Villa Mansi, Villa Torrigiani,
Villa Oliva, Villa Grabau, Palazzo Pfanner,
Giardino dei Tarocchi), Tiziana Grifoni,
(Orto Botanico, Villa Bibbiani, Cetinale,
Geggiano, Castello di Brolio, Abbazia
di Coltibuono, Fonterutoli), Arianna Bechini
(Giardino Garzoni and Parco di Collodi).

For technical consultation:
Giovanni Bartoli

Cover page: The garden of Villa Gamberaia

www.giunti.it

© 2001 Giunti Editore S.p.A.
Via Bolognese 165 - 50139 Florence - Italy
Via Dante 4 - 20121 Milan - Italy

Reprint	Year
7 6 5 4 3	2009 2008 2007

Printed by Giunti Industrie Grafiche S.p.A. – Prato

Contents

Introduction

Tuscany boasts an extraordinary number of villas and gardens. From the 15th century on, gardens were created for palaces or more often villas, in both city and countryside, practically without interruption. This is a region where nature merges with art, the past with the present. A garden calls for great care and attention; maintaining it is frequently expensive. Ancient gardens in particular, those that everyone would like to see, are hard to keep up and often difficult to visit. But to find the 'key' to the garden, to enter a world so wonderful, always fully compensates for the minor difficulties encountered.

The heritage of Tuscan gardens is invaluable both for quantity and for the vast range of chronology and types, spanning a period stretching from the Middle Ages to our own day and embracing situations that are totally different in form, significance and inspiration.

Visiting the gardens of Tuscany is thus a journey in time as well as in space. First comes the Medieval monastic garden, as exemplified by the herb garden of Coltibuono, designed for the monastery's kitchen and pharmacy, where plants were grown not only for their properties but also for their religious and symbolic nature. Next came the first villa garden in the modern sense, exemplified by that of the Trebbio Castle in Mugello. The Medieval herb garden model began to change, becoming more refined, with much longer pergolas, adorned by stone capitals, and perspectives opening out to find a new relationship with the surrounding landscape. But it was only with the creation of the Medicean villas, at Fiesole, Careggi and Poggio a Caiano, that the modern model for a garden was established – a place that is both botanical collection and outdoor museum, adorned with ancient and contemporary works of art. The new villa garden fit harmoniously into the landscape, according to the suggestions of Leon Battista Alberti's *De re aedificatoria*, a famous treatise written in the mid-15th century. The Piccolomini palace garden at Pienza, apparently a walled Medieval garden, a *hortus conclusus*, in reality opens onto the valley in highly innovative manner, testifying to the new humanistic sensitivity.

The 16th century Medicean gardens at Castello, Boboli and Pratolino formed models imitated all over Europe. At the time of the Grand Dukes the garden became an image of political power, assuming complex allegorical meanings, often expressed in grottoes and nymphaeums. Orchards, *ragnaie* for bird-catching, and *boschetti*, or little groves of trees, imposed form on gardens embellished by flowers. Water, essential for irrigation, was collected in ponds or basins and used in various ways for *giochi d'acqua*, or waterworks. Water is the element on which a garden lives, and from which every splendid effect derives. In 1599 the Flemish painter Justus Utens depicted the Medicean gardens in famous lunettes, fixing their image in that golden age which seems to represent the highest peak of Tuscan horticulture.

In the history of the art of gardening, Florence is not the only city in Tuscany to display masterpieces. Gardens based on precise canons but distinguished by different and entirely original materials, types and botanical species were created in the State of Lucca, independent of Florence. In the Sienese territory, subjected to Florence, magnificent examples of garden art have survived from the 16th and 17th centuries, many of them created by Baldassare Peruzzi, the architect who designed such masterpieces as the villa and garden of Vicobello.

In the late 17th and early 18th century the fashion arose for architectural, perspective gardens, designed together with the villa to form a consistent, scenic whole. This was the time of the Baroque garden masterpieces such as Villa Garzoni and Villa Gamberaia. These are of different scenic impact: the first is monumental, the second arouses a sense of intimacy. The model of the terraced garden reappeared in the mid-18th century in the Capponi garden at Florence, and elements of the 16th century garden, the fruit orchard and the *ragnaia*, returned again during this same period in the villa garden La Quiete in Florence. Still in the 18th century the beautiful Val d'Esse, in the Cortona region, assumed the rationalizing aspect still to be seen today, with the flourishing of gardens of agricultural type, incorporating farm structures within them (a fine example is the Passerini garden at Pergo).

The vogue for the romantic garden, derived from the English landscape garden, came late to Tuscany, but was no less significant for this reason. The first masterpieces, the Corsi garden and the Torrigiani garden, appeared in Florence. But the entire region was swept by the naturalist orientation of the English garden and nature, but nature always recreated by the gardener's art. Many Medicean parks, such as those of Castello and Petraia, were transformed in keeping with the new style, and Pratolino became the most important landscape park in Tuscany. In the Lucca region as well Baroque gardens underwent major changes, often due to the Napoleonic domination and intense contacts with contemporary French culture. The new landscape park of Villa Marlia, one of the finest in Italy, harmoniously co-exists with the older gardens. It was in the romantic period that the vogue for botanical collecting swept through Tuscany. The Lucchese collections of trees became famous, with camellias the pride of the area. In Florence too horticulture was promoted by numerous collectors and expert gardeners.

The early 20th century marked the revival of the Italian formal garden. Cecil Pinsent, the English landscape architect, was responsible for the most extraordinary reinterpretations of the Renaissance and the Baroque garden, at I Tatti and at Villa Le Balze in Florence, and at Foce in Chianciano. In the 1930s the young Pietro Porcinai was already active in this field. Born in Florence, he is undoubtedly the greatest Italian landscape artist of the 20th century, the first to rediscover the garden of Italian tradition and reinterpret it in a modern sense. From him came the concept of a sober, functional garden, inserted in the landscape and composed of hedges like the Italian formal garden, but modeled in new forms. Some of his most striking and complete creations are the garden of the Apparita in Siena, that of Villa il Roseto in Florence, and the villa garden Il Castelluccio at Santa Croce sull'Arno. In the decade of the Nineties contemporary art gardens were created. At Celle the romantic park was transformed by systematically inserting contemporary works of art to be displayed outdoors, in harmony with the environment. At Seggiano, near Grosseto, a sculpture garden was created by the Swiss artist Daniel Spoerri; in Maremma, on the border between Tuscany and Lazio, Niki de Saint Phalle created the garden of the Tarocchi; and within the Sterpaia park a number of works by Marcello Guasti were installed.

Lastly, the English tradition of great gardening still lives today in Villa Massei, at the gates of Lucca, allowing us to hope for a revival of the figure of the landscape gardener.

And tomorrow...

Mariachiara Pozzana, May 2001

NOTE. The gardens described in this guide have been selected on the basis of factors such as accessibility to the public, historical and botanical importance, beauty, contemporary realization, and state of conservation. Some gardens have been excluded since they cannot be visited. The difference between gardens described at length and those described briefly indicates no difference in value, but is based only on the above considerations. In the case of botanical gardens, now scientific institutions, that of Florence has been described in greater detail, those of Pisa and Lucca more briefly.

The gardens are presented in three sections, concerning three different geographical areas: *Florence within the walls*, *Florence outside the walls*, and *In Tuscany*. Maps show the locations of the gardens and itineraries for visitors.

Most of the articles consist of two parts, one introductive, the other descriptive. Itineraries for visits are also indicated. The boxes beside each article give information on how to reach the garden, how to visit it and the services provided (for private gardens, this information is based on the owners' statements. In villas inhabited by the owners, visits are allowed at the discretion of the residents). Other boxes are dedicated to the history and particular aspects of the garden: descriptions by famous authors, nature of the botanical collections and so on. For the gardens rich in history, chronological data are given. At the end is a list of texts for those who want to know more about the garden.

STAZIONE F. S.
S. M. NOVELLA
(Stazione Centrale)

PALAZZO DEI CONGRESSI

PALAZZO DEGLI AFFARI

Cenacolo di Fuligno

SAN MARCO

Cenacolo di S. Apollonia

PIAZZ S. MARC

GALLERIA D.ACCADEMIA

Via del Ponte alle Mosse

Via Belfiore

Viale Fratelli Rosselli

Via Luigi Alamanni

Via della Scala

il Prato

PIAZZALE DI PORTA AL PRATO

5

6

Via della Scala

Via B. Rucellai

Via degli Orti

Oricellari

Via Magenta

Montebello

Via Solferino

Via Palestro

Corso Italia

Via Palazzuolo

Borgo Ognissanti

Montebello

Lungarno Amerigo Vespucci

FIUME ARNO

Lungarno di Santa Rosa

PONTE AMERIGO VESPUCCI

Pisana Porta S. Frediano

Lungarno Soderini

Borgo San Frediano

PIAZZA DI VERZAIA

PIAZZA DE' NERLI

Viale Ludovico Ariosto

Viale A. Aleardi

S. FREDIANO

PIAZZA DEL CARMINE

SANTA MARIA DEL CARMINE

PIAZZA TORQUATO TASSO

Via Villani

Via dell'Orto

Via di Camaldoli

Via del Leone

Via de' Serragli

Via S. Agostino

Viale Francesco Petrarca

Via del Campuccio

Via della Chiesa

Via delle Caldaie

Via Maggio

S. SPIRITO

PIAZZA S. SPIRITO

Via Romana

Borgo Tegolaio

S. Felice

PIAZZA DI S. FELICE

Museo Zoologico (La Specola)

4

3

PIAZZA S. FRANCESCO DI PAOLA

Via del Casone

Via Ugo Foscolo

LIMONAIA

Vasca dell'Isola

Porta Romana

Viale della Meridiana

Viale dei Cipressi

Viottolone dei Platani

MUSEO D. PORCELLANE

Anfiteatro

1

Vasca del Forcone o Vivaio di Nettuno

PALAZZO PITTI

KAFFEEHAUS

GROTTA DEL BUONTALENTI

CORRIDOIO VASARIANO

PIAZZA DE' PITTI

Via del Guicciardini

S. FELICITA

PIAZZA S. FELICITA

S. MARIA SOPRARNO

PONTE VECCHIO

Borgo S. Jacopo

Via Toscanella

FORTE DI BELVEDERE (San Giorgio)

2

Via di Belv

Porta San Giorgio

Costa di San Giorgio

PIAZZA DE' M

Villa San Leona

STAZIONE

PIAZZA DELLA STAZIONE

SANTA MARIA NOVELLA

PIAZZA S. MARIA NOVELLA

OGNISSANTI

PIAZZA D'OGNISSANTI

S. Pancrazio

PIAZZA CARLO GOLDONI

Via della Vigna Nuova

PONTE ALLA CARRAIA

PIAZZA DI CESTELLO

PIAZZA N. SAURO

Lungarno Corsini

S. Trinita

PONTE S. TRINITA

Lungarno Guicciardini

Lungarno degli Acciaiuoli

PAL. DAVANZATI

PIAZZA D. SIGNORIA

PAL. VE

PIAZZA S. FIRENZ

BADIA FIORENTINA

GALLERIA DEGLI UFFIZI

Lung. A.M.L. de' Medici

Lungarno Ger

Lungarno Torrigian

Lungarno ALLE GRAZ

PON

Via de' Panzani

PIAZZA DELL'UNITÀ ITALIANA

Via de' Cerretani

PIAZZA DELLA REPUBBLICA

Via de' Tornabuoni

PAL. STROZZI

Via Pellicceria

Via de' Calzaiuoli

Via del Corso

V. de' Pecori

BATTISTERO

PIAZZA DEL DUOMO

S. MA DEL FI

Via del Proconsolo

Via Roma

Via d. Condotta

Via Por S. Maria

SAN LORENZO

PIAZZA D. MERCATO CENTRALE

OPIFICIO PIETRE I

PAL. MEDICI RICCARDI

Via de' Martelli

Via de' Pucci

Via Cavour

Via de' Ginori

Via de' Gori

Via San Gallo

Via San Zanobi

Via Guelfa

Via Taddea

Via Panicale

Via Nazionale

Via Faenza

Via Fiume

Via Guelfa

PIAZZ S. MARO

10

Florence within the walls

Boboli

A living work of art

HOW TO ARRIVE

In the immediate vicinity of Ponte Vecchio.
Address: Piazza Pitti 1
Buses: 11, 36, 37, D
tel.: +39 055 265171
Sept.-Oct.: 8:15 am -
5:30 pm / Nov.-Feb.:
8:15 am -3:30 pm /
Mar.-Apr.: 8:15 am -
4:30 pm / May: 8:15
am - 5:30 pm /
June-Aug.: 8:15 am -
6:30 pm
Closed Jan. 1, May 1,
December 25, the first
and last Monday of
the month.
Admission: 2,00 €
Rest rooms - Bookshop
Café-restaurant

Detail of the
amphitheater

Boboli is known the world over as one of Italy's most important gardens. So famous that its name alone evokes the idea of a Renaissance garden, Boboli is one of the peak achievements in the Italian art of gardening.

The park as we see it today is chiefly the result of two initiatives; first the 16th century garden behind the Pitti Palace was created, then, between 1630 and 1631, the cypress avenue designed by Giulio Parigi was planted.

The construction of the Medicean garden began when Eleonora, wife of Cosimo I, purchased land known at the time as the 'Pitti garden' from the name of the first owners.

Niccolò Pericoli, known as Tribolo, was commissioned to design the garden. The sculptor based its layout on the perspective axis that traverses the entrance to the palace and rises along the hill behind it. In place of what remained of a stone quarry he built an amphitheater divided by *ragnaie* and lined with fruit trees. To the left of the palace a great flower garden was planted.

Numerous artists worked on this magnificent garden. When Tribolo died he was succeeded by Davide Fortini, then, between 1554 and 1561, by Giorgio Vasari followed by Bartolomeo Ammannati (from 1560 to 1583). After 1574 Bernardo Buontalenti was also summoned by Francesco I to work at Boboli.

In the early 17th century Cosimo II decided to extend the garden beyond the bastions erected during the war with Siena. Giulio Parigi, commissioned to enlarge the gardens in 1612, created the cypress avenue. Parigi transformed the garden amphitheatre behind palazzo Pitti into a theatrical space built of masonry in 1630; the work was finished by Alfonso Parigi the Younger.

After some years of abandonment work on the garden resumed in 1765, at a time when the Grand Duchy had passed to the Hapsburg Lorraines.

At the initiative of Pietro Leopoldo the *Kaffeehouse* was built (1775) as well as the *limonaia* by Zanobi Del Rosso (1777-1778) and the Palazzina della Meridiana by Niccolò Gaspero Paoletti (1776).

In the 19th century the Annalena entrance was built, with a *palazzina* and grotto, and a major

change was made in the garden, consisting of destroying the old mazes to make room for the carriage drive designed by Pasquale Poccianti (1834).

Boboli is the model for the garden-museum, a garden created to display ancient and modern statues. It can also be considered the exemplification of a perfect manual on garden art, due to the multitude of elements that, over the course of

The Isolotto

the centuries, have gone to make up this extraordinary work of art. Along the garden's two main axes – the 16th century one that crosses the amphitheater and goes on to the statue of *Abundance*, and the 17th century one of the cypress avenue – the visitor is struck by examples of garden art as numerous as they are splendid. Outstanding among them are the late 18th century *Kaffeehaus* garden, the turf theater around the Forcone pool and the little Baroque garden of the Cavaliere.

In front of the Palazzina della Meridiana is a second turf theater, dramatically dominated by the marble *Pegasus* (coming from the Pratolino park) and a small rose garden in the vicinity of the little Madama grotto, with its imposing statue of *Jove*.

Important elements of garden architecture are the great hedges lining the paths through the ancient *selvatici*, or wild areas, and the *ragnaie* in the 17th century part of the garden, a particularly fascinating section of the park.

The Isolotto in the center of its pool is a splendid Baroque garden on water, created to display potted citrus trees.

For its complex layout and the great number of works of art all over the garden, two different itineraries for visitors are suggested, each of them to be covered in two to three hours.

13

First Itinerary
From the Ammannati courtyard to the Great Grotto *by Buontalenti*

Behind the severe facade of the Pitti Palace the garden opens out in all its splendor. Closed off by the Moses grotto (which takes its name from the porphyry statue of *Moses*), the Ammannati courtyard forms an elegant entrance to the park. The grotto was designed to solve the problem of linking spaces on different levels, since the courtyard is lower than the amphitheater behind it. The ramp of stairs to the right of the grotto leads up to the **amphitheater** leaving to the left, above the Moses grotto, the fountain of the Artichoke, a work by Francesco Susini (1639-1641). In front of the fountain is a little geometric garden, from which can be admired the perspective that unites the different levels of the garden, running across the amphitheater and the **Forcone pool** to arrive at the tiered turf theater and the statue of *Abundance*.

At the center of the amphitheater

The *Kaffeehaus*

Statue of Abundance

Garden of the Cavaliere

Forcone pool

Kaffeehaus

Grotticina di Madama

Amphitheater

Fountain of the Artichoke

Buontalenti's Great Grotto

Ammannati's courtyard

Moses Grotto

Palazzina della Meridiana

is a large granite pool placed there in 1840 by Poccianti and the Egyptian **obelisk** coming from Villa Medici, erected in Boboli by Paoletti in 1790. The amphitheater has six tiers of seats in masonry surmounted by a decorated balustrade. Originally, 24 niches held classical statues with figures of dogs and other animals at the sides. In 1818 Giuseppe Cacialli renovated the amphitheater, placing terracotta urns with imitation marble decoration between the statues. On the steep slope that leads to the

At left
A work by
Igor Mitoraj
in the garden

The Palazzina
della Meridiana

Fountain of the
Mostaccini

Pool of the
Isolotto

The Forcone pool

Botanical
garden

Cypress
avenue

Limonaia

Meadow of the
columns

The grottoes

The most significant element of the Renaissance grotto may be the fact that it is a concrete place of encounter between art and science. It was in the grotto that the most exotic and curious combinations of materials were experimented. The *Grotticina di Madama* and the *Great Grotto* of Boboli are among the first garden grottoes to be built in Italy (the *Great Grotto* is now undergoing restoration). Constructed through a highly complicated technique, exposed to the erosive effect of water and thus requiring frequent maintenance operations, the two grottoes provide exceptional documentation on the cultural and artistic environment in which 16th century gardens were created, an environment where science and natural philosophy, aesthetic caprice and enchantment were interwoven to form a fascinating whole.

Above
The Great Grotto

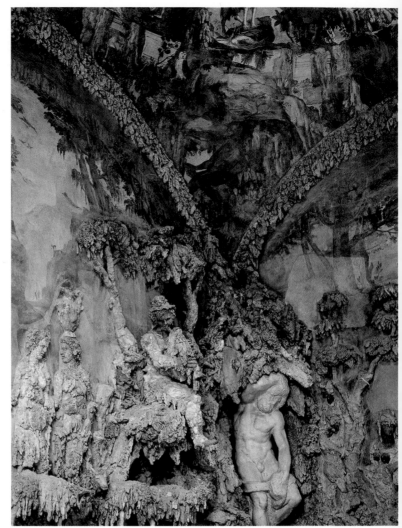

Forcone basin (a semicircular lawn links the first two levels, at the exit from the amphitheater) are the classical statues of a *Togaed Personage*, the *Emperor* and *Ceres*.
The path leads up to what could be called the second amphitheater, built of tiers of turf seats and bounded by plane trees pruned to the shape of candelabras. At the center is the great mixtilinear pool designed by the architect Zanobi Del Rosso (1777-1778), who transformed an existing 16th century pool to build this one, used to col-

lect water to irrigate the garden. The bronze statue of *Neptune with Naiads and Tritons* by Stoldo Lorenzi dates from 1565-1568. The central stairway ends at the marble statue of *Abundance*, sculpted by Giambologna in collaboration with Pietro Tacca and Sebastiano Salvini. The allegorical figure clearly symbolizes the prosperity of the Grand Duchy.
From the statue of *Abundance*, after having admired the splendid panoramic view over the city, the garden and the palace, turn right

to find the **garden of the Cavaliere** (from the name of the bastions erected by Michelangelo in 1529). The little formal garden, in the past planted to medicinal herbs, was rearranged in 1612 by Giulio Parigi, who filled it with rare species. On the same occasion, the big room for vases that now houses the Porcelain Museum was constructed. Today the garden, planted to roses and peonies, is splendid at the flowering season, in late April and early May. Its current design

den in front of the *Kaffeehaus* was originally an orchard. From the central path a number of ancient ilexes can be seen on the right. These great trees are all that remains today of the imposing 16th century *ragnaia*. At the end of the path stands the fountain of *Ganymede* by Stoldo Lorenzi (c. 1550). Continuing to the right along a straight path, we see on the right the marble statue of *Jove* coming from Pratolino. The path leads on to the **Grotticina di Madama**,

is the work of Giuseppe Del Rosso, who also built the stairway with the ancient statues of the Muses in 1792.

From the garden of the Cavaliere we return to the statue of *Abundance* and descend toward the *Kaffeehaus*, with the imposing walls of Forte di Belvedere on the left. This elegant little building, commissioned by Pietro Leopoldo di Lorena and designed by Zanobi Del Rosso, reflects the Central European fashion of the times for drinking coffee outdoors. The fine gar-

which can be visited only with permission. Commissioned by Eleonora di Toledo of Davide Fortini and built between 1553 and 1555, the little grotto is distinguished by animal sculptures emerging from the back wall, the work of Baccio Bandinelli and Giovanni Fancelli. Returning to the broad avenue we descend still further to find Buontalenti's grotto, called the *Great Grotto*, a real chamber of wonders designed to strike the beholder with amazement (now being restored). This building, begun by Vasari

The Forcone Pool, also known as the 'Neptune fishpond'; in the background, the Pitti Palace

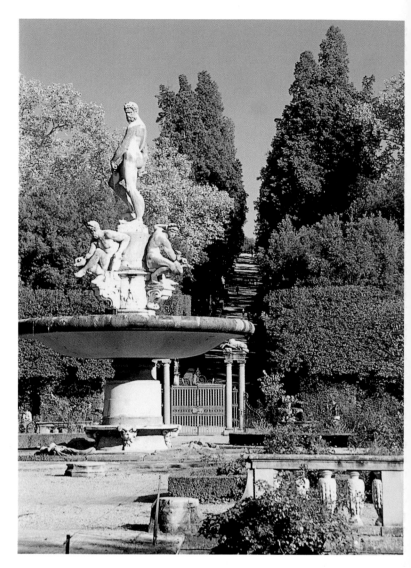

The fountain
of *Oceanus;*
in the background
the cypress avenue

between 1556 and 1560, was transformed into a rustic grotto by Buontalenti (1583-1593). Along with the Grotticina di Madama it became the model for every grotto built later. The facade is decorated with *spugne*, stuccowork (*Peace* and *Justice* by Giovanni Battista del Tadda) and statues (*Bacchus and Ceres* by Baccio Bandinelli, 1552-1556). Inside, in half-shadow, figures modeled in stucco, perhaps inspired by the myth of Pyrrhus and Deucalion, seem to

emerge from the walls. In the corners two of Michelangelo's *Slaves* struggle to free themselves from the block of marble (these are copies; the originals are now in the Accademia Gallery). Before the grotto is the exit from the garden, known as the *rondò di Bacco* from the marble statue of the *Young Bacchus* by Valerio Cioli (a plaster cast of the original, known also as *Nano Morgante*, is displayed). Not far away are the Roman statues of the *Dacian Prisoners.*

Second itinerary

From the level of the amphitheater to the 'meadow of the columns'

From the amphitheater lawn we turn right, descending toward the Palazzina della Meridiana by Paoletti and Poccianti. To the right of the palazzina a small camellia garden can be seen from above. From here the path leads up to the right, arriving in the vicinity of the Botanical Garden, open only in summer. The garden, created by Filippo Parlatore between 1841 and 1850 to replace the 18th century *jardin potager* (of which only the pineapple greenhouses remain) has lovely ponds where aquatic plants grow. Through the *cerchiata* of ilexes, a majestic corridor of trees planted between 1612 and 1614, we arrive at the cypress avenue. Descending along the avenue we see on the left the remains of the 17th century mazes, demolished in 1834 to make room for the carriage drive.

The fountain of the Mostaccini, situated along the Medieval city walls, marks the boundary of the *ragnaia* of *Peace*; decorated with sixteen stone mascarons, the fountains was probably created by Romolo Ferrucci between 1619 and 1621. The avenue is lined with classical and late 16th century statues. Near the end of the avenue are 17th century sculptures representing various games. We then arrive at the famous **pond of the Isolotto**. An artificial island, elliptical in shape, is laid out as a formal garden with potted lemon trees, antique roses and bulbs and the fountain of *Oceanus* by Giambologna (1576). We then go on to the so-called 'meadow of the columns'. In the vast semicircular space that closes off the garden to the south, Paoletti placed two column; twelve classical busts adorn the hemicy-cle. Further on are a group of 17th century sculptures of grotesque subject, the *Caramogi* by Romolo Ferrucci.

From the broad meadow we turn to the right, rising along the avenue that goes back to the Palazzina della Meridiana. On the left is the great *limonaia* built by Zanobi Del Rosso between 1777 and 1778. It is still used today to shelter the five hundred urns of citrus trees in winter. In front of the *limonaia* is a lovely formal garden with antique roses and bulbs. Beyond the *limonaia* a path leads, on the left, to the Annalena grotto, the most recent of the Boboli grottoes. Constructed in 1817 by Giuseppe Cacialli, the grotto contains the *Adam and*

Eve sculptural group by Michelangelo Naccherino (c. 1616). From here visitors can either exit onto Via Romana or return to the *rondò di Bacco*.

The 'meadow of the columns'

To know more

F.M. Soldini, *Descrizione del giardino di Boboli*, Florence 1789.

Boboli '90, Proceedings of the international symposium of studies for safeguarding and valorizing gardens, Florence, 9-11 March 1989, Florence 1991. Vols. I and II.

The vegetation in the garden

In Boboli, trees, hedges, meadows and flowers are elements of extraordinary interest and enchanting beauty. Cypress avenues and *cerchiate* of majestic ilexes, green walls that harmoniously delimit space, hedges of box in elaborate geometric patterns, all concur to make the garden not only a living work of art but also an invaluable document of the history of gardening in Italy. The maintenance of Boboli calls for great effort and professional expertise. Many sections of the park have been restored recently and new plants have been added or used to replace old ones; for example, antique bulbs in the garden on the Isolotto and camellias in the little garden visible from the Palazzina della Meridiana.

The *Pegasus* and the turf theater

Chronology

1549 Eleonora di Toledo, wife of Cosimo I, purchases the 15th century Pitti Palace, already possessing a garden of modest size. The project for the new garden is commissioned of Tribolo who completes, in the words of Giorgio Vasari, "the layout of the mount... accommodating all of the things with fine judgement in their proper places".
1550 Davide Fortini succeeds Tribolo at the death of the latter. The work goes on.
1553-1555 The Grotticina di Madama is constructed.
1574 Buontalenti is appointed director of works in Boboli.
1583-1593 The *Great Grotto* is built.
1599 Justus Utens paints a lunette that documents the appearance of the garden at the time.

1630-1634 Giulio Parigi and his son Alfonso transform the 'garden amphitheater' into a building. The garden is extended to the south toward Porta Romana. It now includes the 16th century bastions erected under Cosimo I. The cypress avenue, the labyrinths, the *ragnaie* and the pool with the Isolotto are built.
1636 The statue of *Abundance*, begun by Giambologna and finished by Tacca, is placed in the position it still occupies today.
1637 The statue of *Oceanus*, a work by Giambologna, adorns the Isolotto.
c. 1637-1641 Francesco Susini creates the fountain of the *Artichoke*, placed above the Moses Grotto.
1737 The Botanical Garden is created, linked to the museum of nat-

ural history 'La Specola'.
1766 The *jardin potager*, or cutting garden, is created, famous for its pineapple greenhouse.
1774-1775 The *Kaffeehaus* is built to the design of Zanobi Del Rosso.
1777-1778 An orange house is built to replace the old seraglio. Changes are made in the pool surrounding the fountain of the Forcone.
1790 The Egyptian obelisk is placed at the center of the amphitheater on a base designed by Niccolò Gaspero Paoletti.
1796 The 'meadow of the columns' is laid out.
c. 1834 The broad carriage drive is inaugurated. A large portion of the 17th century maze is transformed into *boschetti* in English landscape style.

Giardino Bardini

A marvelous surprise

To the visitor walking along the Lungarno in the vicinity of Ponte alle Grazie there appears, beyond Palazzo Mozzi and on the square of the same name, a thicket of vegetation: the Giardino Bardini. Entering the garden, following in your imagination the antiquarian Stefano Bardini as he decides where to place sculptures, passing beyond the great wall that opens onto Costa San Giorgio, is an intensely gripping experience. The visitor feels himself almost suspended in the air over the city, viewed from above, so near but yet so far. From here those domes, those spires, those walls appear almost within reach, at our fingertips.

Not many years ago this garden was still a tribute to the gardener's excellence. Scattered over the perfectly trimmed lawns were vases of azaleas, displaying a collection that was the pride of the garden. The baroque stairway rose steeply, opening out before the visitor like a triumphal procession between stone statues and borders of iris and roses. Views of the Florentine countryside with its olive groves and meadows alternated harmoniously, reminding us that the utopia of the country within the city can exist for brief seasons. The deep shade of the *selvatico*, or wilderness, offered shelter from the blazing heat of summer.

Today, observing nature prevail over the work of man, the images of the past overlap and alternate with those of the present, allowing us imagine how this place of delight, bounded by Medieval walls and the Arno River, will appear

HOW TO ARRIVE

Take the street that leads from Ponte Vecchio to Forte Belvedere. Managed by the Fondazione Parchi Monumentali Bardini e Peyron, promoted by the Ente Cassa di Risparmio di Firenze.
Address:
Costa San Giorgio 4, 6
tel.: +39 055 2612214
Visiting hours: the garden is now undergoing restoration. Visits are limited to the spring.

The belvedere loggia overlooking Florence

At right
Two statues before
the belvedere loggia

after restoration, with its splendid panorama over the city.

This great garden rich in historic memories is located in the heart of Florence. It is a garden composed of three distinct parts, hard to identify today but clearly legible on the basis of historical documentation; and lastly, it is a work of art about to recover its lost identity.

Itinerary of visit

Imagine that the visit starts from the future entrance on Piazza dei Mozzi, opening onto the lower part of the garden. Leaving on the left a bed of box clipped in curious Art Nouveau shapes, we continue up a little slope, with the system of roofs and terraces distinctive of Palazzo Mozzi behind us to the left. The **wall-fountain** with decorations in *pietra spugna*, marble tesserae and shells almost certainly forms part of the 18th century layout of the area behind the building.

Continuing to the right we find another great backdrop wall decorated with the Mozzi coat of arms. The high wall supports the terraces at the top of the Baroque stairway, to the left of which appears a large niche with architectural elements in stone. Within it is a marble statue put together by Bardini out of ancient fragments (to make room for a new road connecting the lower part of the garden and Palazzo Mozzi with the villa facing on Costa San Giorgio, Bardini decided to have the Medieval orchards destroyed. The walls we see today are built of debris from this demolition).

Continuing to the left we come upon the arches of the *limonaia* enlarged by Bardini. A graceful stairway bounded by spiral scrolls (perhaps added by the antiquarian) leads to a rustic grotto. From here the road goes up to the 19th

A stone vase
on the upper lawn

Agricultural area

Ceres and
Bacchus

English
garden

Rustic
grotto

Belvedere
loggia

Tempietto

A stone dragon in the pond

Baroque
stairway

Grotticina

Limonaia

Lower
garden

The *Ceres and Bacchus* group on the upper lawn

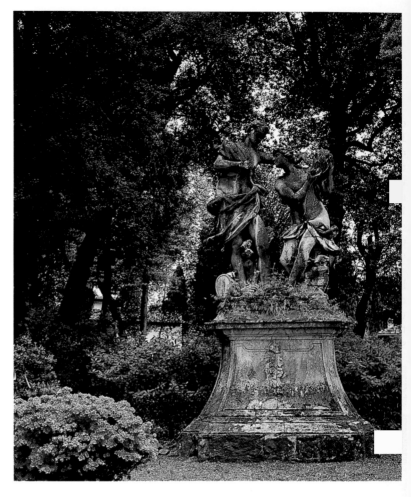

The restoration of the garden

The Bardini garden is now undergoing restoration after having been abandoned and closed for nearly thirty years. What is described here is the garden as it is today, and not as it will be a few years from now, with renovated structures and new vegetation. The great stairway will become a flower garden again, as it was in Baroque times. Overlooking the city there will be a garden theater for outdoor performances. Two large orchards will occupy the now-abandoned areas used in the past for agriculture. Lastly, azaleas will come back to embellish the upper part of the English-style woods. Although the garden will have to be closed while this restoration is being carried out, the Ente Cassa di Risparmio di Firenze, responsible for the project, has decided to open it to the public in springtime.

century *berceau* that embellished the last portion of the Baroque stairway. Continuing along the carriage drive we reach a crossing with the stairway path. From this broad space there is a splendid view of the city.

We can either wander deeper into the thick woods of ilex and laurel or continue to the left, along the straight path that runs through the agricultural part of the garden.

Amid olive trees and meadows we reach the top of the garden, arriving at the lawn before the **belvedere loggia** and the agricultural area just below the 16th century Ginevra bastions. A steep monu-

mental stairway also leads to the lawn on which the loggia stands. The wall on the western side of the stairway, which separated the Mozzi property from the neighboring one, conserves important remains of the Baroque layout with its decorated backdrops and niches, and probably waterworks as well.

An inviting path running along the wall starts from the loggia lawn. From here the great buttresses of the Medieval walls encapsulated in the bastions can be seen. Returning to the belvedere loggia we find on the left a little rustic grotto that was part of the 19th century layout

View of the
agricultural area

Below
Spring flowers

designed by Giacomo Luigi Le Blanc. Standing before it is one of the garden's most important trees, a centuries-old **ilex** that dominates and frames the panorama over Florence.
From here the paths and meadows of the English landscape garden designed by Le Blanc lead up to the villa enlarged by Bardini. Some of the decorative elements that belonged to the 19th century hydraulic system, composed of a sinuous, elongated pond, low water falls and waterworks, can still be seen here. Numerous other ele-

ments were added by Bardini to create various scenes, such as the sculptural group of *Ceres and Bacchus* and the marble fountain (composed of both original and reintegrated elements).
The terrace at the back of the villa is adorned by myrtle bushes clipped in ornamental shapes. From here we descend along a winding path, leaving behind us the *tempietto* with its low waterfalls, and exit at last onto Costa San Giorgio.

Chronology

1309 The Comune of Florence intends to buy the Mozzi property located in the Popolo di Santa Lucia de Magnoli. A document in our possession describes a palace "with great loggia and garden behind said palace and adjacent house with orchard and meadow, and walled earth behind the house".
c. 1400 Due to severe economic problems the Mozzi are obliged to sell the family palace.
1551-1552 Luigi di Conte di Giovannozzo de' Medici again becomes owner of part of the palace and also purchases the area behind it which forms the western sector of the Bardini garden.
First half of the 17th c. The architect Gherardo Silvani builds for Giovan Francesco Manadori a villa in a panoramic site on Costa San Giorgio, with a garden.
1781 The Mozzi property is enlarged by the donation of a "house with large orchard" by Margherita D'Orford to Giulio

Mozzi. Margherita bequeaths him all of the property in her possession (including Villa Medici at Fiesole).
Before 1793 Villa Manadori is bought by the Cambiagi family.
1819 Giacomo Luigi Le Blanc becomes the owner of Villa Manadori and the land surrounding the building. He creates a modern English landscape park.
1839 Pier Giannozzo de' Mozzi purchases the Le Blanc property.
1880 The estate is purchased by the Silesian Princess Wanda Carolath-Benthen.
1913 The antiquarian Stefano Bardini buys the whole property and renovates the buildings.
1922 At Bardini's death the property passes to his son Ugo.
1965 Death of Ugo Bardini. The Bardini heredity enters a lengthy bureaucratic and administrative process which has only recently concluded. The Ente Cassa di Risparmio di Firenze promotes and finances its restoration.

25

Giardino Corsi

(or Annalena)

The semicircular
bench

Between the Torrigiani garden and the Boboli park is a small English garden, covering an area of barely half a hectare, filled with the surprises and artificial perspectives typical of the landscape fashion that swept Florence in the first half of the 19th century. The garden is distinguished by a broad elliptical bed with elaborate parterres of box and neo-classical elements. The words engraved on the marble plaques and stone bench emphasize the philosophical and contemplative atmosphere of the garden. Clipped hedges of laurel and viburnum and great trees – ilex, cedar and magnolia – envelop the visitor in a rarified atmosphere populated by terra-cotta statues, originally covered with stucco to imitate marble.

The origins of the garden date back to the 15th century, when the area formed part of an ancient orchard owned by the Annalena nuns. The present-day garden was however laid out between 1801 and 1810 by Giuseppe Manetti, commissioned to create it by Marchese Tommaso Corsi, who had recently become the owner of the property.

In 1544, during the war against Siena, Cosimo I had ordered a line of fortifications to be built within the existing walls of Oltrarno. The area coinciding with the present-day garden was gutted and split in half by the line of bastions. When the new wall was demolished in 1571 the land remained abandoned, cluttered with an enormous pile of earth and bricks for over two centuries. The property was

still in this condition when Manetti started to create the new garden. One of the most brilliant and innovative landscape artists in Florence at that time, he utilized the huge mass of debris with great ingenuity to create a number of features culminating in the terrace facing on Via dei Serragli. By doing so he managed to transform the little space available into a fascinating

garden, boasting a collection of plants that was famous among the botanists of the day.

Itinerary of visit

To establish an itinerary for the Corsi garden seems almost to contradict the intention of the designer who, in an area of restricted size, ingeniously created an atmosphere where the visitor can lose himself, forgetting that he is in the heart of the city.

To best appreciate the garden, walk around the outer edge and observe the neo-classical entrance on Via Romana with the two images of dancing girls, the Loggetta del Canto (on the corner between Via Ro-

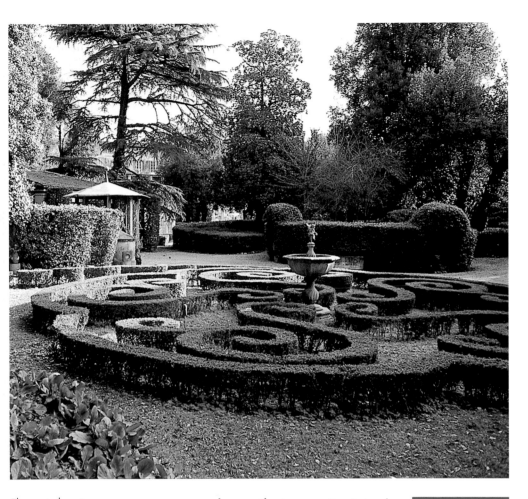

The central *parterre*

mana and Via del Moro), the statue of *Mercury* and the bass-relief with winged figures. These elements were carefully placed by Manetti to delimit the inner space and accentuate its isolation from the city. The *boschetto*, or small wooded area, visible above the wall that runs along Via dei Serragli, has a similar function.

Once inside the garden, let yourself be guided by the feelings aroused by the vegetation and furnishing elements. Stroll along the path that winds through the trees; observe the terra-cotta statue in the laurustrine niche and pause to rest on the semicircular bench decorated with elegant neo-classical designs (the same designs appear on the facade of the villa). Near the elliptical **bed** on which the garden centers is a spacious aviary and further on, toward the boundary wall, appears the building of the *limonaia*.

A stone inscription praises friendship and the words engraved on the stone bench remind the visitor that "the wise must submit to fate". The severe inscriptions appearing throughout the garden remind us that it was conceived for silence and meditation.

Annalena

The name of Annalena derives, according to tradition, from Anna Elena, daughter of Galeotto Malatesta and wife of Baccio d'Anghiari, killed in a conspiracy plotted by Cosimo the Elder. Anna Elena, now a widow, retired to monastic life, founding a cloistered order that was named Annalena after her.

Giardino Torrigiani

A romantic park

The Torrigiani garden, one of the largest gardens located within the walls (covering an area of seven hectares) is perhaps the most important romantic park in the city. This extraordinary creation fully expresses the aesthetic and philosophical ideal of the English garden, whose landscape model, in contrast to the architectural one of the Italian and French garden, developed in Europe during the 18th century and began to spread through Italy near the end of the century.

The project by Luigi de Cambray Digny, a highly cultured architect of French origin, dates from 1813. The owner Pietro Torrigiani had decided to create a garden itinerary steeped in Masonic symbolism.

This is alluded to by the statues of the sphinx and of *Osiris* and the numerous architectural structures scattered over the park, such as the tempietto of Arcadia or the Torrino, placed to mark the most significant points. But the Masonic symbols were to remain mysterious and hard to decipher. Not even the *Guida del Giardino Torrigiani*, published in 1824, was able to explain their meanings. What is instead apparent today are the aesthetic principles, reflecting the art of the English landscape garden: elegantly designed winding paths, broad meadows where flocks of sheep once grazed, artificial hillocks that animate the composition, conferring on it variety and profundity, majestic woods of rare and precious trees (the original plans called for a fine botanical collection as well).

Itinerary of visit

Visitors enter from the gate on Via dei Serragli. On the right the stat-

At right
Sculptural group with lion attacking a bull

Next page
The circular lawn looking toward the Torrino

Below
The tempietto of Arcadia

ue of *Osiris*, the Egyptian god of death and resurrection, holds up two tables bearing rules for visiting the garden. "Dogs are not allowed, nor are horses and carriages", we read. "Do not touch the flowers, plants, or minerals. No games allowed without special permission. Walk only on the paths". To the right of the entrance a column commemorates the work of the botanist Pietro Micheli. At the end of the avenue stands the remarkably elegant villa in neoclassical style. On each side of it are formal gardens. The one on the right, next to the great *limonaia*, is adorned with beautiful **marble vases**. The one on the left is situated beside the nursery with greenhouses for indoor plants. Strolling along the right-hand path we pass

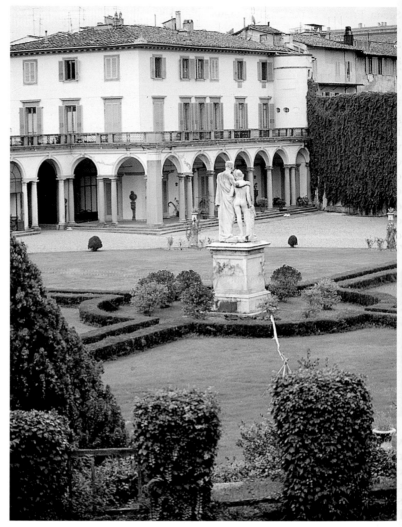

This page
The circular lawn
and the villa

Next page
Interior view of a
greenhouse

At right
A statue in the garden

before a *boschetto* of bamboo and then arrive at the tempietto of Arcadia. Inside the tempietto is a sculptural group representing a lion attacking a bull.

Continuing along the paths bounded by hedges of laurel and other evergreens we reach a broad circular **lawn** in front of the villa, also known as the 'cavallerizza', since it was originally designed as a place to race horses. Furnished with benches, vases and statues, this lawn is the ancient core of the property.

At the center of the lawn is a statuary group of remarkable size. Sculpted by Pio Fedi in the 19th century, it portrays *Seneca pointing the way to the young Pietro Torrigiani*. On the Via del Campuccio side is a gymnasium.

The semicircular back, in the form of a theater, and the end building with its elegant neo-classical lines, now used as a small apartment, can be seen. We go on to climb the hillock built of debris from the 16th century earth bastions that defended Florence in the war against

Siena. From here there is fine view of the garden below. On the hillock are a Chinese balance (an exotic game), an aviary and the famous **Torrino**, created by the architect Gaetano Baccani and inspired by the heraldic emblem of the Torrigiani family.

It was used as astronomical observatory and library. In the lower part of the garden, on the left, an extraordinary centuries-old beech and other unusual trees testify to the exceptional botanical importance of the garden throughout the 19th century.

Turning toward the level ground

we encounter first, on the right, a dry ditch (recalling the project, never carried out, for bringing abundant water to the garden); then, still on the right, tennis courts. A little further on are the splendid stables; near them, on the southern side, the nursery greenhouses.

To know more

M.P. Maresca, *Il giardino Torrigiani*, in "Arte dei Giardini. Storia e restauro", 1993, II, pp. 55-77.

Web: www.giardinotorrigiani.it

Chronology

1531 Raffaello Torrigiani purchases an orchard and two houses located on the southern side of Via del Campuccio. This was to be the original core of the garden.

1571 The bastioned front built in 1544 for the war against Siena is demolished. The 'casino Torrigiani' is built.

End of 16th c. The Dominican Friar Agostino del Riccio describes the garden, praising its abundance of vegetables, variety of citrus fruits and jasmines.

17th c. Carlo Torrigiani and Camilla Strozzi enlarge the *casino di delizie*.

1716 The illustrious botanist Pier Antonio Micheli creates a garden in which to experiment with growing rare plants.

1802-1817 Pietro Torrigiani extends the property. The architect Bernardo Fallani is commissioned to enlarge the *casino* on Via del Campuccio.

1813 Pietro Torrigiani commissions Luigi de Cambray Digny to renovate the garden. The architect is a member of the Masonic lodge 'Napoleone', to which Torrigiani also belongs. Cambray Digny abandons the project after only one year.

1819 The architect Gaetano Baccani is called to direct the works in the garden. He creates the neogothic tower, the imitation battlements on the Medicean bastions, the gymnasium, the aviary and several other *giochi*. In the same year the first inventory of the plants grown in the garden is published, edited by Antonio Pucci. The inventory lists 13,000 plants in the ground and 5,500 in vases.

1841 The second catalogue of the plants grown in the garden is published, edited by Antonio Targioni Tozzetti.

31

Giardino Corsini
al Prato

The triumph of geometry

The geometric
parterre

The beauty of the Corsini garden, entirely concealed to the view by the facade of the palace on the Prato, is breathtaking. In spring the flowering of pink and red rockrose, lavender, roses, peonies and cherry trees shows this to be one of the rare Florentine historical gardens that is well preserved today.

Elegant lemon urns and solemn marble statues contribute to the sober elegance of the whole. The landscape designer Oliva di Collobiano is responsible for the recent selection of flowers and aromatic herbs planted in great variety in the beds.

Bounded by hedges of box, they contain ancient examples of *Poncirus trifoliata*, a thorny species of citrus fruit used for particularly intricate hedges.

The history of the garden began in 1591 when Alessandro Acciaiuoli, already the owner of a house famous for its garden, purchased the land and commissioned Bernardo Buontalenti to build a palace. The work was not finished due to financial difficulties, and the "large house begun and not finished, with a garden and a *ragnaia*" was sold in 1621 to Filippo di Lorenzo Corsini.

Filippo commissioned the architect Gherardo Silvani to finish the *casino di delizia*.

The garden annexed to Palazzo Acciaiuoli was not very large, but was extended by purchasing adjacent land. Gherardo Silvani designed a layout with sophisticated geometric divisions of the design in the center.

Enlarged by Gaetano Baccani between 1834 and 1836, the *casino al Prato* became the residence of Neri Corsini, Marchese of Laiatico, and Eleonora Rinuccini.

Itinerary of visit

The garden is entered from the Prato, through the great doorway for carriages.

The beauty of the geometrical *parterre* with its box hedges, beds

of flowers and aromatic herbs, strikes the visitor with wonder and delight. Along the sides of the *parterre* are two English *boschetti*, designed in romantic style and created in the early 19th century, distinguished by great ilex and laurel trees.

The ground is covered by a carpet of acanthus. It is probable that one of the two *boschetti* was created by transforming an ancient *ragnaia* of ilex trees.

Next we find the avenue along the sides of which Cardinal Neri Corsini (1685-1770) placed an important antiquarian collection of classical inscriptions and marbles. Perpendicular to the loggia, the avenue divides the central portion of the garden in half.

The statues, standing on tall bases, create a fine perspective effect, conferring greater depth on the view. At the end of the avenue are two perfectly conserved *limonaie*, containing ancient tools for the cultivation of citrus trees.

In spring there is a splendid flowering of pink peonies in front of the *limonaia* on the left; and an equally beautiful flowering of cherry trees before the one on the right.

Il Prato

A lready by the Middle Ages the Prato d'Ognissanti had assumed fundamental importance in defining the urban structure of Florence. It was not a city square or *piazza*, but rather a great unpaved area, kept as *prato*, or meadow, and used for games, performances, horse races, and so on. In the frenetic traffic of the city it is hard to imagine today the ancient calm of the broad Prato. In the 16th and 17th centuries fine palaces were built around the Prato, the most imposing of them Palazzo Corsini, which conceals behind its facade one of the richest and best conserved gardens in Florence.

The garden looking toward the palace

Beyond the *limonaie* a door opens in the encircling wall onto Via della Scala.

After having crossed a lawn where ancient linden trees stand we find on the left the wall that separates the garden from a broad meadow and fruit orchard. This is the part of the garden that most resembles open countryside. Its rural aspect reminds us that, in the original design, the garden was to be a place capable of uniting ornamentation and cultivation of the land, knowledge of the useful and art of the delightful.

Orti Oricellari

The grotto of Polyphemus

HOW TO ARRIVE

In the immediate vicinity of the Santa Maria Novella railway station.
Owner: Cassa di Risparmio di Pisa / Mr. and Mrs. Ridomi
Address: Via Orti Oricellari 9
Buses: 1, 2, 9, 16, 17, 29, 30, 33
tel.: +39 055 2398071/211638
Visiting hours: by appointment upon presentation of request in writing to the Cassa di Risparmio di Pisa, Via della Scala 85, 50123 Florence (to the attention of the Director). Accessible to the disabled
Restrooms
(The other half of the garden owned by Mr. and Mrs. Ridomi, with entrance on Via Bernardo Rucellai, is now undergoing restoration and is hard to visit at present.
For information telephone +39 055 2302212).

The city block between Via della Scala, Via Rucellai, Via Palazzuolo and Via degli Orti Oricellari encloses a part of what was one of the most complex and refined gardens in Florence. Conceived as a place of philosophical *otia* by Bernardo Rucellai (from which derives its name) in the early 16th century, the garden became the meeting place for literary figures, humanists, philosophers and historians such as Machiavelli, Zanobi Buondelmonti, Jacopo da Diacceto, and Luigi Alamanni. Near the end of the century the Orti Oricellari were purchased by Bianca Cappello, and parties and games took the place of academic debate. The garden was transformed; first dedicated to philosophic meditation it now became the place of amusement and delight. Bianca, the mistress of Francesco I de' Medici, entertained her friends with per-

fidious tricks. Clelio Malespini reports that there was a hole dug in the ground, concealed by wooden boards covered with grass, which opened like a trapdoor to receive the shocked guests who fell in. Awaiting the unlucky ones at the bottom of the hole were thirty pages wearing devils' costumes. But this was the only unpleasant surprise. Later, having recovered from the shock, guests were welcomed to the *loggetta* by "beautiful girls, entirely nude under golden mantles, superbly adorned, which lightly and barely concealed their secret parts, covered with pearls, diamonds, rubies and sapphires, and drenched in perfume from head to foot".
Redesigned by Alfonso Parigi and Ferdinando Tacca for Giovan Carlo de' Medici around the middle of the 17th century, the garden was transformed into a park in the second decade of the 19th century by Luigi de Cambrai Digny, commissioned by Giuseppe Stiozzi Ridolfi. The architect inserted the existing elements of the 17th century garden into a larger, more complex design, inspired by the philosophical and progressive ideals of Masonry. The

The grotto under the palace

Next page
The statue of *Polyphemus*

themes common to the romantic garden were thus developed in the Orti Oricellari.

Itinerary of visit

From gate on the Via degli Orti Oricellari the statue of *Polyphemus*, sculpted in plastered masonry by Antonio Novelli, a pupil of Giambologna, can be seen. The garden is divided into two properties, making it hard to understand the original project, in which the statue and the grotto of Polyphemus were placed one before the other.

In the section nearest to Via della Scala the garden is dominated today by the statue of Homer's giant. In the other part of the garden a group of 17th century grottoes can be visited. The **Grotto of Polyphemus** (or *antro dei Venti*) is decorated with *spugne*; an artificial hillock was built to house it. In the Grotto of the Baths, decorated with calcareous concretions, are bucolic images now ruined by time and humidity. Beyond the balustrade that separates the beds of the Villino Cesaroni, facing on Via Rucellai, from the park can be glimpsed the neoclassical facade of the *Pantheon* by De Cambrai Digny. Restored in the 1860s by Giuseppe Poggi, the building contains tombs and relics of the illustrious men who frequented the garden at the time of the *Sylva Oricellaria*. The 17th century *grotto* located below the palace is magnificent, with niches decorated with shells and calcareous *spugne*.

To know more

L.M. Bartoli, G. Contorni, *Gli Orti Oricellari a Firenze: un giardino, una città*, Florence 1991.
VV. AA., *Il gigante degli Orti Oricellari*, Rome 1993.
M. Pozzana, *Giardini di città*, Florence 1994, p. 77 and ff.
E-mail: Dip35@caripisa.it
Tit35@caripisa.it

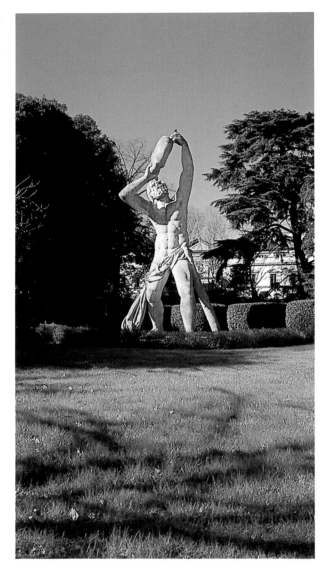

Chronology

1481-1489 Bernardo Rucellai and Nannina de' Medici, his wife, purchase land in the vicinity of Porta al Prato.
Early 16th c. A *casino di delizia* with garden is built, the beginning of the Orti Oricellari.
1573 The property is bought by Bianca Cappello.
1641-1657 The Orti Oricellari become the property of Giovan Carlo I de' Medici.
1670 Ferdinando Ridolfi purchases the property and commissions Pier Francesco Silvani to enlarge it.
Early 19th c. Giuseppe Stiozzi Ridolfi requests Luigi de Cambrai Digny to design for him an English landscape park.
Last decade of the 19th c. The garden is divided into two parts. Ferdinando Cesaroni buys the western part and builds two houses with access from Via Rucellai.

35

Giardino Budini Gattai

A collection of camellias

HOW TO ARRIVE

Between Piazza San
Marco and Piazza SS.
Annunziata, behind the
Accademia Gallery.
Owners: The Budini
Gattai family
Address:
Via de' Servi 51
Buses: 6, 31, 32
tel.: +39 055 210832
fax: +39 055 212080
Visiting hours:
by appointment only,
closed in August.
Guided visits in the
months of March and
April for the flowering
of the camellias; in the
month of May for the
flowering of the aza-
leas.
Admission: 6,00 €
Accessible to the
disabled
Rest rooms

The best time to visit the garden is undoubtedly spring when, around the end of March, the camellias blossom in splendid profusion. This collection, one of the few remaining in Florence, boasts plants of ancient variety and remarkable size.

Entering from the great doorway on Piazza SS. Annunziata the visitor passes through the half-shadow of a monumental portico into this little 16th century jewel set in the heart of Florence.

Ugolino Grifoni, the secretary of Cosimo I, had chosen this strategic site on which to build his palace and had commissioned Bartolomeo Ammannati to design it. The famous sculptor and architect worked on it, starting in 1563, for over ten years, creating a geometric garden of modest size but abounding in significance and decoration. A fountain with the statues of *Jason with sea monsters* and *Venus*, described in 17th century texts, was the most striking feature of the garden, along with the espaliers of citrus trees and evergreens what marked off the space according to customary Florentine tradition.

The fountain of Venus

In the 18th century the garden was enlarged, the fountain moved, and in its place was built a wall-fountain to hold the statue of *Venus*.

In the late 19th century the garden became the property of the Budini Gattai family and underwent further transformation, entirely losing its old geometric layout to assume a new romantic guise.

During the same period the singular **banana grove** (*boschetto*) was planted in a small, protected courtyard; here the trees have found an ideal microclimate.

The collection of camellias, which has now become a real *boschetto*, was then planted in front of the loggia opening onto the garden. It contains, among other varieties, the double-flowered *Callista*, the splendid *Mutabilis Traversii* bearing double flowers with white petals streaked and bordered in red, and the *Terzjana* developed in Milan in 1845 and named in honor of Marchesa Terzi.

On an axis with the loggia is the rustic decoration fountain with the statue of *Venus* and the marine creatures that originally adorned the 16th century fountain. At the lower left, built into the wall of the palazzo, is a stone recording the date when the work was completed: 1574.

To know more

M. Pozzana, *Il giardino di palazzo Grifoni*, in "Bartolomeo Ammannati Scultore e Architetto, 1511-1592", edited by Niccolò Rosselli del Turco and Federica Salvi, Florence 1995, pp. 155-160.

E-mail: info@budinigattai.com

Web: www.budinigattai.com

The garden with its camellias looking toward the palazzo

The *boschetto* of banana trees

37

Orto botanico
The *'Giardino dei Semplici'*

At left
The central fountain

At right
Interior of a greenhouse

Next page
Springtime flowering

Created around the middle of the 16th century, the Florentine Orto Botanico is a garden of rare characteristics. Although conceived with scientific intentions, it was created according to the same principles of beauty, variety and elegance deemed valid for any oth-

er garden designed in the same period. It is a garden of knowledge, where the plants must be observed, a garden linked to the university world; but at the same time it is a place of recreation and delight.
It was the idea of Luca Ghini, famous physician and naturalist, professor at the University of Bologna, to let students enrolled in the faculty of Medicine study live medicinal plants. From Ghini's idea originated the first Botanical Garden, in Pisa. In 1545, at the recommendation of Ghini himself, Cosimo I decided that Florence too should have a botanical garden open to students of medical botany. From this decision came the *Giardino dei Semplici*, the third oldest of its kind, after the botanical gar-

dens of Pisa (1543) and Padova (1545).
The project was commissioned of Niccolò Pericoli known as Tribolo, who proposed an irregular rectangular layout with an octagonal island at the center. The island was to be adorned by a marble fountain and surrounded by a moat crossed by mobile bridges. Starting from the island eight paths originally subdivided the garden into eight spaces of more or less triangular shape. The triangular sections were in turn divided into

elegant geometric sections of small size, each of which contains varieties of plants to be studied. At the four sides of the garden are small *boschetti*.

Itinerary of visit
The layout of the garden today is quite different from the original plan, although the spatial organization into 'squares' divided by two broad crossing avenues, centered around a fountain, has been retained. The shape of the 'squares' and the secondary paths derives instead from transformations dating from the middle of the 18th century. The garden now has the shape of an irregular polygon. During the 19th century a rectangle of land was added on the eastern

side, toward Via Capponi. From the entrance on Via Micheli (the original entrance was on today's Via La Pira) visitors accede to the eastern side of the garden to find themselves in front of glass greenhouses, the so-called *stufini*, which house a fine collection of orchids. The large greenhouses built of masonry contain the most important collections in the Orto, including rare and exotic plants: **cicas**, **cactuses**, and **ferns**.

In the northeast corner is the pond. On the Via La Pira side are long, narrow beds containing the rich collection of **medicinal plants**. In the opposite corner is an artificial hillock with ponds for aquatic plants. The rectangle of added land, which looks on Via Capponi, houses numerous conifers, including interesting examples of bald cypress (*Taxodium distichum*) with grotesque pneumatophores, above-ground roots emerging from the water through which the trees absorb oxygen.

The various sections of the garden are occupied by trees, some of them centuries old, and by numerous shrubs and herbaceous plants, each identified by a label bearing the common name and the Latin one, the botanical family to which it belongs and the zone of origin of the species.

A visit is particularly pleasant in spring, when the splendid collection of azaleas standing along the main paths is in full flower.

To know more

P. Luzzi, F. Fabbri, *I tre orti botanici di Firenze*, in "I Giardini dei Semplici e gli Orti botanici della Toscana", edited by S. Ferri and F. Vannozzi, Perugia 1993.
www.ortbot.it

Chronology

1545 Cosimo I de' Medici rents land from the nuns of the Convent of San Domenico del Maglio. The Orto Botanico of San Marco is created.
1662 The first catalogue of the plants grown in the Orto is published.
1718 Cosimo III appoints the illustrious botanist Pier Antonio Micheli director of the garden.
1783 The Orto is assigned to the Accademia dei Georgofili.
1801 Management of the Orto is entrusted to Ottaviano Targioni

Tozzetti, who orients the garden's collections toward botanical studies again.
19th c. A rectangular area is added on the Via Capponi side and heated greenhouses are built.
Early 20th c. The library and collections of 'La Specola' museum of natural history are transferred here.
1929 Through an agreement between University and Municipality, the Orto becomes a public garden.

39

Il giardino del Museo archeologico

The fascination of ruins

HOW TO ARRIVE

In the vicinity of Piazza SS. Annunziata.
Address: Via della Colonna 38
Buses: 6, 31, 32
tel.: +39 055 235750
Visiting hours: Saturday 9:30 am-12:30 pm, guided visits every 45 minutes - Admission: 4,00 €, reduced 2,00 € (18-25 years old). Free admission for under 18 and over 65 Accessible to the disabled, rest rooms and bookshop

The garden of the Archaeological Museum is a narrow rectangular plot where flowers and colors are concentrated to form a kind of barrier against the pressure of the city. This is the garden of the Crocetta Palace, transformed in the early 20th century into an original collection of archaeological monuments of various provenance which, according to the ambitious project of Luigi Adriano Milani, were reconstructed in the garden and inserted into a new context. The history of the garden began when Lorenzo the Magnificent purchased several houses in the area, planning to build a colossal urban villa surrounded by gardens. The project, which was to have been directed by Giuliano da Sangallo, was never carried out because the nearness of the Ospedale degli Innocenti and three other important religious structures, the Crocetta Monastery, the Angiolini Monastery and the Church of Santissima Annunziata made the place more suitable to religious retreat than to the construction of *casini di delizia*.

When Cosimo II decided to enlarge the building, the garden was, in fact, adapted to the usage imposed by a cloistered life. The side walls were raised and the neighboring houses lowered to ensure maximum privacy to occupants of the garden. At the end of the garden a small chapel was then built. In the first half of the 18th century the Prince of Craon rearranged the space bounded by the walls and

Francesco Romoli, the Boboli gardener, created twelve *parterres* cultivated to citrus trees and vineyards, in the most classic tradition of Medicean gardens. A large room for citrus trees was also built. The layout with rectangular beds survived up the 19th century, when it was changed by the introduction of a circular motif that transformed the two quadrangular sections nearest the palace. After having temporarily housed the Court of Accounts at the time when Florence was capital of Italy, the Crocetta Palace was chosen in 1879 as the site of an Archeological Museum in which ancient sculptures coming from the Uffizi and various villas would be placed.

After the failure of several projects of this kind, Luigi Adriano Milani proceeded to create a garden closely linked to the museum, in which to place sculptures and architectural monuments coming from archaeological excavations. From 1900 to 1903, assisted by the architect Giuseppe Castellucci, Milani reconstructed a number of Etruscan tombs in the garden. This project, linked to other interesting experiments in the outdoor exhibition of archaeological material, has the merit of providing Florence with a museum itinerary inserted in a garden, important in spite of its small size.

Itinerary of visit

From the loggia of the palace, today the site of both the Archaeological Museum and the Department of Archaeology, visitors enter the garden. The circular pond survives from the original layout. On the right we find the tomb of the Diavolino (7th c. BC) coming from Vetulonia, reconstructed in 1901-1902, and another tomb from Vetulonia with an inscription bearing

Tomb of the Crucifix of Tufo

Tomb of Casale Marittimo

the name of the deceased carved on the lintel. On the left is the tomb of Tlesnei, with barrel ceiling, reconstructed in 1899.
Further on, to the right, is the Inghirami tomb, a faithful copy of the tomb discovered at Volterra in 1861 containing 53 alabaster funerary urns. Before the tomb stands a majestic **centuries-old yew tree** with thick green foliage. Dispersed among the vegetation and the bright colors of the seasonal flowers are the tomb of Veio (7th c. BC) and the tomb of Casale Marittimo, with circular cell; before the latter is the so-called 'lion of Tuscania'. Near the tempietto is the tomb of the Crucifix of Tufo, the altar and *favissa* (votive grave) from Bolsena. In the western part of the garden are two modern greenhouses.

The ancient yew tree

To know more
Il Giardino del Museo archeologico nazionale di Firenze, edited by Antonella Romualdi, Florence 2000.

Flowers in the Baroque garden

The tulip arrived in Europe in the mid-16th century. The vogue for collecting flower bulbs swept through European gardens in the following centuries, when garden owners were infected by the so-called 'tulip craze' of the times.

Donated by a German diplomat to the botanist Carlo Clusio around 1570, the tulip became the most precious flower bulb in the Netherlands within a few years. Expert hybridizing soon produced varieties grown with petals of various shape – pointed or fringed, 'parrot's crest' or double, multicolored or

in the garden of the Orti Oricellari. We are shown anemones in full flower and coronary anemones, fritillaries, hyacinths, narcissus tazzetta, narcissus 'of the poets', and narcissus pseudonarcissus (buttercups), tulips in great variety, with the predomination of 'parrot' tulips.

All of the Medicean gardens boasted flowers that sometimes cost a fortune. During the 18th century bulbous flowers were superseded by herbaceous plants. The flowering of the former, although magnificent, lasts in fact only a very brief time.

Flowering
of antique bulbs

streaked. The tulip was not alone to populate 17th century gardens; numerous other bulbs were ardently sought after and collected. Their fascination can be felt again in looking at the miniatures by Giovanna Garzoni, commissioned by Cardinal Giovan Carlo de' Medici. They are splendid 'portraits' of flowers meticulously described and perfectly recognizable, displayed in splendid vases, either glass or blue-and-white Chinese porcelain. Nothing more than Garzoni's miniatures gives an idea of how splendid the flowering season must have been, at the time,

Flowering of
Narcissus tazetta

Camellias

The camellia, known also by the name 'Japanese rose' is an evergreen shrub with beautiful dark green glossy leaves, which may reach the size of a tree. Its scientific name is *Camellia japonica* and the plant belongs to the family of the *Theaceae*. Tea is in fact made from the leaves of a particular variety of camellia, the *Camellia sinensis*.

The first camellia introduced into Italy was the 'Celebratissima', cultivated in the Reggia of Caserta around 1760. In the late 18th and early 19th centuries the camellia spread throughout central and northern

did camellia garden, the Borrini nursery at Sant'Andrea di Compito, in the Lucchesia, produces a remarkable number of varieties, as does the Tesi nursery at Pistoia. The *boschetto* of camellias at Villa Mansi in the Lucchesia displays the varieties *Camellia japonica* 'Lefevriana'(1841), *Camellia japonica* 'Carlotta Papudoff' (1861) and *Camellia japonica* 'Giuseppina Mercatelli' (1880). At Villa Torrigiani are splendid examples of *Camellia japonica* 'Fimbriata' (1816) and *Camellia japonica* 'Imbricata alba'. Again at Florence, in the Budini Gattai garden, we find the dou-

Italy. There were numerous camellia collectors in Florence in the 19th century; during this same period camellias were also very popular in the area around Lucca.

The flower can have innumerable magnificent shades of color, from pure white to pink to red, with a great variety of stripes, spots and dotting. The multifold shapes are classified under three headings: simple flowers, semi-double (with corolla irregularly imbricated, that is petals arranged without order in the form of an anemone or that of a peony), double (they may be irregular, star-shaped or spiraling). There is a wide range of sizes, from 6.5 cm to about 13 cm in some varieties grown today. The plants usually flower in springtime, although the royal *Camellia sasanqua* blossoms in all its splendor in autumn. For some years now, thanks to the exhibitions held at Pieve di Compito, in the Lucchesia, and in the Budini Gattai garden in Florence, the camellia has returned to attract the interest of flower-lovers; numerous varieties are again being cultivated.

In the vicinity of Villa Borrini, famous for its splen-

ble-flowered *Callista*, the splendid *Mutabilis Traversii* bearing double flowers with white petals streaked and bordered in red and the *Terzjana*, created at Milan in 1845 and dedicated to Marchesa Terzi.

To know more
G. Cattolica, A. Lippi, P.E. Tomei,
Camelie dell'Ottocento in Italia, Lucca 1992.

Above
Camellias in a garden near Pistoia

At left
Camellia japonica, semi-double marbled

Florence outside the walls

Giardino Capponi

The most beautiful view of Florence

HOW TO ARRIVE

In the vicinity of Piazzale Michelangelo, near the Arcetri astronomical observatory.
Owner:
Maria Teresa Benedetti
Address: Via del Pian dei Giullari 3
Bus: 11
tel.: +39 055 2298609
fax: +39 055 223465
Visiting hours: upon presentation of request in writing and only for groups of at least 10 persons. Guided visits.
Admission: 10,00 €
Partially accessible to the disabled
Restrooms

The rear facade of the villa extends in its severe elegance along the road front. Villa Capponi has always exerted a special fascination over the visitor, transmitting a sense of calm solemnity, perhaps impossible to achieve today in designing a garden. Contribut-

den, and the rose garden, skillfully laid out around the house and bounded by walls with fine scroll decorations.

The different areas have been created at different times: the secret garden, located below the terraced level on which stands the villa, was laid out in the late 16th century, probably by the owner Gino Capponi.

It links in emblematic manner the different levels of the house in its higher position and the countryside below. At the same time con-

The lawn
in front of the villa

ing to the remarkable effect of the whole are the perfect proportions of garden and villa, the balance between closed and open spaces, the fluid communication between the different levels, between countryside and house. The garden is composed of a great lawn in front of the house and three smaller levels, in reality three outdoor rooms: the lemon garden, the secret gar-

nections between the different levels are ingeniously created by an underground passage that leads from the semi-basement level to the secret garden. The citrus garden was created later, in 1774, by Ferdinando Carlo Capponi, who demolished a portion of the *selvatico*, or wilderness, and planted 1,600 small box bushes. In the 19th century the garden underwent no major changes. In 1882, when the property was bought by Lady Scott of Ancrum, the villa probably had the appearance of a neglected jewel. Although it had lost its economic importance as a small farm it was fascinating to the eyes of its new owner. Lady Scott added the second walled garden below the secret garden, linking them by a stairway in masonry. This rose garden reiterates the ornamental theme of the walls in the upper garden, but also utilizes tall cypress hedges clipped in topiary shapes

to design a swimming pool for the lower part of the garden. The new initiative did not change the existing aspect, since Pinsent decided to surround the pool with high cypress hedges, and to place stone statues around it.

A new outdoor room was thus created, ensuring privacy for swimming and sunbathing. Pinsent completed the vegetation along the country road beneath the terraced lawn in front of the house. He may also have designed the topiaries standing against the front facade

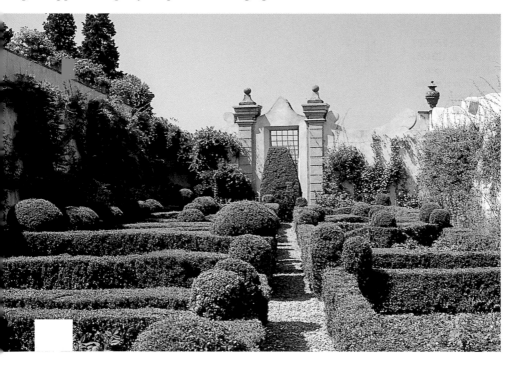

o make the composition more striking. Lady Scott also made changes in the facades of the villa, adding the two loggias and, presumably, closing the semi-underground corridor and transforming it into a rustic grotto.

The garden continued to evolve. Henry Clifford, who bought the villa in 1928, commissioned the English landscape artist Cecil Pinsent

of the villa and the others placed before the window in the secret garden.

Itinerary of visit

From Via del Pian dei Giullari we enter the half-shadow of the doorway giving on the lawn. A stone gate opens onto the path that ideally extends into the countryside below. The roadway, little more

The secret garden

The lawn in front
of the villa, with a view
of Florence

A statue beside
the swimming pool

At right
The lemon garden

than a path that runs along the wall of the terraced lawn, is bounded by hedges of lilac and bordered with iris.

The stone portal is dominated by two terra-cotta griffons. At the sides, slightly recessed, two terra-cotta lions bear a coat of arms. Beyond the portal, to the right, we enter the lemon garden, encircled by **decorated walls**, where flowerbeds of myosotis bordered with box surround the potted citrus trees. In line with the entrance portal, against the back wall, is a stone basin. On the right, behind the straight wall, stand cypresses and ilexes, what remains today of the original *selvatico* demolished in the 1770s to make room for the new garden.

The garden is canonically divided into four sections, each of them further subdivided into beds of box embellished by magnificent lemon urns. Returning to the lawn, we continue up to border of the terrace overlooking the **secret garden**. From here there is an unforgettable view of the city.

We then descend a stairway to find the enclosed, intimate space of the flower garden with its abundant blossoming of silene. Behind us is the little grotto, or grotticino, created in the late 19th century by closing the ancient semi-underground corridor that leads to the kitchen. Nearby is a small stone pool used to irrigate the garden. The rectangular space is surrounded on all four sides by decorated walls. A window opens out in the west wall, giving a view of Pian dei Giullari.

Through a portal with iron gate we descend to the lower garden, or rose garden. Tall **cypress hedges** form walls of vegetation rising almost as high as the outer walls. Before a great semi-circular hedge of yew are three stone benches.

Now we go down through the ancient circular entrance lined with cypress hedges to find Pinsent's swimming pool.

Inspired by Renaissance pools and fountains, it reiterates the theme of the mascaron spraying a jet of water, as well as the decoration scheme with statues and benches placed in alternation along walls of vegetation.

Following the charming rural path we go back up toward the stairway leading to the terraced lawn. In the early years of the century, perhaps at the initiative of Pinsent himself, cypresses and box hedges clipped in spherical shape were planted along the paths that lead from the garden into the countryside.

To know more

M. Pozzana, *Una guida per conoscere Villa Capponi*, Florence 2000.

Cecil Pinsent's swimming pool

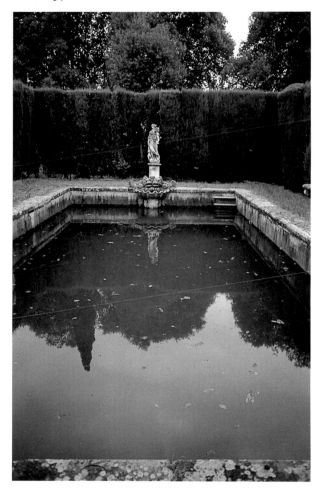

Chronology

1568-1572 Gino di Lodovico Capponi and his wife Maddalena Benci purchase property situated in the Popolo of San Leonardo in Arcetri. The first core of Villa Capponi is built, then enlarged and embellished with a garden.
1765 Ferdinando Carlo Capponi inherits the villa and makes sweeping changes.
1882 The Capponi family sell the villa to Lady Scott. She creates the third secret garden, conceiving of it as a particular rose garden. She also adds to the villa loggias built with sandstone columns coming from the demolition of the *Mercato Vecchio* (Old Market) of Florence.
1928 The villa is bought by Henry and Esther Clifford. Henry Clifford, curator of the painting section of the Philadelphia Museum of Art, has met Cecil Pinsent through his friend Bernard Berenson, and commissions him to design the swimming pool, finished in 1930.
1978 The Cliffords sell the villa to its present owners.

Villa il Roseto

Modern Renaissance

HOW TO ARRIVE

In the vicinity of Piazzale Michelangelo, near the Arcetri astronomical observatory. Privately owned. Visiting hours: by appointment only and for groups of max 25 persons. tel.: + 39 055 570216 (Università internazionale dell'arte, Centro studi sul giardino e sul paesaggio)

The great Florentine landscape designer Pietro Porcinai (1910-1986) worked on Villa il Roseto in the early 1960s, at the peak of his artistic and creative career, producing a garden that is undoubtedly one of his masterpieces.

The inspiring theme of this villa is a reference to the tradition of gar-

entered from the street. The ample entryway is designed to serve a number of functions.

It is a salon for parties but also a garage, monumental entrance and simple place of access, with walls plastered in the combed pattern of the past, like those running along Tuscany's country roads, and a pebbled pavement decorated in circular motifs.

An iron-and-stone stairway leads up to the **terraced garden** above, conceived as a garden-sculpture where the circle, the perfect geometric shape, becomes the element

The garden-terrace seen from the circular pond

dens ruled by architectural laws, in keeping with the design of the house, linked to it by perspective and geometric harmony.

Porcinai worked on the building as well, altering its spatial relationships and moving the main entrance to the first floor. Lastly he created, in the manner of Renaissance architects, a hanging garden above the broad area

that generates space. The stone circles in the pavement are bounded and enclosed by circular box hedges.

Along the main axis, centered on the door to the villa, three perfectly linked circles lead to the fountain at the end of the terrace.

The **plane tree** rising against the sky at the level of the hanging garden is in reality planted on the lower level; it existed prior to Porcinai's renovation, but has been conserved through ingenious technical solutions.

A circular stone pool, positioned lower than the hanging garden level, completes the composition, in a quiet space that seems designed for meditation.

From the hanging garden, flanking the building, go on to the **rose garden** situated in an area that still bears the agricultural features of the Tuscan landscape. Country paths lead to the swimming pool

and a tennis court shielded by high hedges of evergreen.

An admirable unity of concept, the harmonious syntheses of geometry and nature distinguish this extraordinary creation which, for its breath of inspiration, recalls the work of the great landscape designers of the most illustrious Tuscan tradition.

The entrance to the villa

Above
The garden-terrace

51

Villa della Petraia

The garden of fruits

HOW TO ARRIVE

Between Sesto Fiorentino and Careggi, in the vicinity of Quinto.
Address: Via di Petraia 40, Castello - Bus: 28
tel.: +39 055 452691
fax: +39 055 452691
Visiting hours:
June-Aug : 8:15 am - 6:30 pm / Sept.-Oct.: 8:15 am -5:30 pm / Nov.-Feb.: 8:15 am - 3:30 pm
Admission: 2,00 €, reduced 1,00 € (18-25 years old and teachers)
Free admission for under 18 and over 65 only if citizens of EU.
Guided visits
Restrooms - Café

Despite the great changes undergone by the Petraia garden, its aspect today is very close to the original one. The garden was laid out in the 16th century over three terraces, the one on the same level as the villa (now known as the *piano della Figurina* from Giambologna's statue of *Venus* that adorns the fountain); the intermediate terrace, with the nursery and flower garden; and the lower terrace, originally a fruit orchard distinguished by two great circular beds. A very clear picture of the garden as it appeared in the late 16th century can be seen in the lunette by Justus Utens depicting the villa with its garden. Although the painter was concerned with details to the point of inserting some imaginary ones, he shows us more clearly than any other source how the garden was constructed. Beside the villa was the little orchard of *'frutti nani'* or dwarf fruit trees.

On the level below was the flower garden with potted citrus trees. On the third level was the great *fruttiera*, or garden of fruit trees, with *boschetti* and *cerchiat*e of ilex-

Above
A topiary against the wall around the *piano della Figurina*

This page
The lower *parterre*

52

es bounding the two flowerbeds. The projects carried out during the course of the 19th century have altered this design in favor of a formal solution appearing today as an elliptical layout with little flowerbeds in the upper part.

The lovely park behind the garden is an important example of Central European landscaping style. Winding paths meander through thick vegetation (fine conifers grow here) with ample views opening onto flowery meadows, a sea of jonquils in Springtime and lovely scenes of the surrounding landscape.

Itinerary of visit

From the gate on Via della Petra-

ia a broad avenue slopes upward to the side entrance, leading directly to the lower terrace through a *boschetto* of ilexes. Next comes a spacious *parterre* sloping gently downhill, divided into beds now planted to dwarf pear trees. Further on are geometric flower beds of elaborate design, providing a fine example of the 19th century flower garden.

Below a great avenue of plane trees bounds the southern side of the garden, while in the center a fountain emphasizes the central axis of symmetry along which the garden is laid out.

A stairway leads to the intermediate level where a rectangular basin holds water used for irriga-

The *piano della Figurina*

53

A hillside covered with villas

Villa Petraia is situated on the slopes of Monte Morello, in a sunny, panoramic position. In the 16th century, at the time when villas first began to be built on these hills, the geometry of the agricultural fields divided into plots by the Romans many centuries before could still be seen. The numerous villas that still today populate the hillside, from the Villa of Castello to the nearby Villa Corsini, from Villa La Quiete to the many private villas all around, testify to the love of the Medici and other Florentine families linked to the Grand Ducal court for this beautiful hillside.

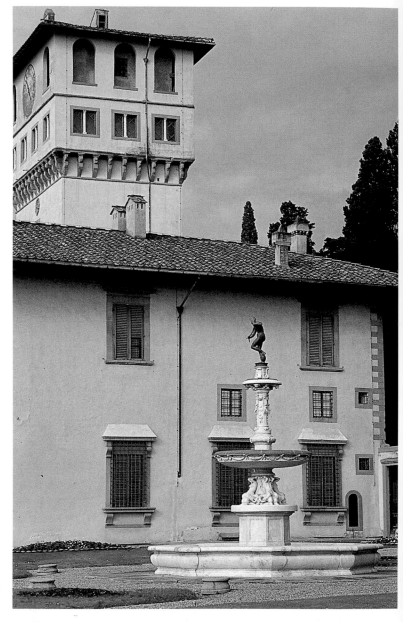

The fountain of Fiorenza and the villa

tion. On the left a **flower garden**, recently recreated, revives the 17th century fashion for flower bulbs and what has been called the 'tulip craze' of the times.

Ideally, the garden should be visited in springtime to appreciate the splendid **flowering** of fritillaries, antique and 19th century varieties of tulips and 'Grand-ducal' hyacinths.

Climb the central stairway again to reach, above the nursery, the level of the villa. On the right can be seen copies of Tribolo's marble fountain with the bronze statue of *Fiorenza* or *Venus* by Giambologna (the original, which was brought

The flower garden

The fishpond

here from the Villa of Castello, is on the first floor of the Villa of Petraia. The marble fountain is now being restored in an adjacent building).

The circular flowerbeds have recently been replanted according to the model of the 'bread basket' flower bed. To the left of the villa is a little woods with fine cedar trees, planted under the reign of the Savoia. Behind the villa an unusual fountain is formed of a great calcareous *spugna*. The path on the right leads to the 19th century **park**, the one on the left to the Villa of Castello.

To know more

C. Acidini, G. Galletti, *Le Ville e i Giardini di Petraia e Castello*, Pisa 1992.
Web: www.ambientefi.arti.beniculturali.it

Chronology

1568 Ferdinando de' Medici begins the work of transforming the villa and garden.
1573-1574 The terraced levels of the garden are constructed.
1588 Grand Duke from 1587, Ferdinando commissions Raffaello di Zanobi di Pagno to resume work on the garden and villa.
1609 La Petraia passes to Ferdinando's son, Don Lorenzo.
1785-1788 The fountain of Fiorenza, built by Tribolo and adorned with a small bronze statue by Giambologna, is moved to the villa from the garden of Castello.

1798-1813 In the years of Napoleonic domination the lower garden is transformed into an elliptical layout with a fountain at the center.
1829 Leopoldo II (1824-1859) begins constructing the great English landscape park, designed by Joseph Frietsch.
1872 The Belvedere is built. The *piano della Figurina* is renovated to the design of Ferdinando Lasinio. The estate, become Savoia property subsequent to the unification of Italy, is the favorite residence of Vittorio Emanuele II and the *bella Rosina*, his beloved.

55

Giardino di Castello

Nature, science and beauty

HOW TO ARRIVE

Between Sesto Fiorentino and Careggi.
Address: Via di Castello 44, Castello - Bus: 28
tel.: +39 055 454791
fax: +39 055 452691
Visiting hours:
June-Aug.: 8:15 am - 7:00 pm / Sept.-Oct.: 8:15 am - 6:00 pm / Nov.-Feb.: 8:15 am - 4:00 pm / Closed the 2nd and 3rd monday of the month.
Admission: 2,00 €, reduced 1,00 € (18-25 years old and teachers)
Free admission under 18 and over 65.
Accessible to the disabled - Restrooms

A splendid white azalea in front of the Grotto of the animals

Castello is the first of the Medicean gardens in order of time, and is perhaps the most fascinating for its magnificence. Between 1537 and 1538 Cosimo I decided to enlarge and improve an estate that had been owned by his family since 1477. Niccolò Pericoli known as Tribolo was chosen to lay out the garden, according to a densely symbolic plan. Built around a central maze of cypresses on a line with the Grotto of the Animals, the garden was designed as an allegory of Medicean good government.

Castello was known as a garden of statues, which numerous artists were called upon to decorate; in addition to Tribolo, Pierino da Vinci, Bartolomeo Ammannati and Giambologna, all of whom remarkably embellished the garden by creating its famous grotto.

In narrating the life of Tribolo, Giorgio Vasari describes the garden of Castello and the complex iconological program traditionally attributed to Benedetto Varchi, a program designed to celebrate the Grand Duchy of Cosimo I as a true golden age. Tribolo was also responsible for the concept of the Grotto of the Animals, on which other artists, including Vasari, worked after his death.

The most consistent changes, apart from the 18th century enlargement of the citrus tree rooms, were made in the 1770s and '80s, when the maze was demolished, the fountain of *Fiorenza* removed (and brought to Petraia) and the entire design of the central portion of the garden was altered. The fountain of *Fiorenza* was replaced by the one with the sculptural group of *Hercules strangling Antaeus* by Ammannati. Later on Leopoldo II created the great English parks of Castello and Petraia and the avenue linking the two villas.

Itinerary of visit

The avenue in front of the villa results from successive transformations of the original one, considered one of the wonders of the villa. It was formed of the great *cerchiata* of mulberry trees that Tribolo had designed to link the villa, in a bold landscaping initiative, to the Arno River.

Access to the garden is found to the left of the main entrance to the villa, now the headquarters of the Accademia della Crusca. The garden appears as an ample walled orchard divided into geometric compartments, and is dominated by the fountain with the statue of *Hercules strangling Antaeus*, surrounded by other marble statues. In springtime great vases of azaleas are placed round the fountain; at its sides are flowerbeds bounded by hedges of box. In spring the flowerbeds are splendid with antique roses, peonies and bulbs. Next comes the lemon garden, recently replanted with citruses in the ground, to be protected in winter according to the tradition of Medicean gardens. On the left are two huge *limonaie*, where the renowned collection of potted citrus trees, numbering over 500, is kept in winter. Go on from here to the **Grotto of the Animals**, excavated in the embankment above which has been planted a *selvatico* (see description of the grotto on

The garden of Castello

The Grotto of the Animals

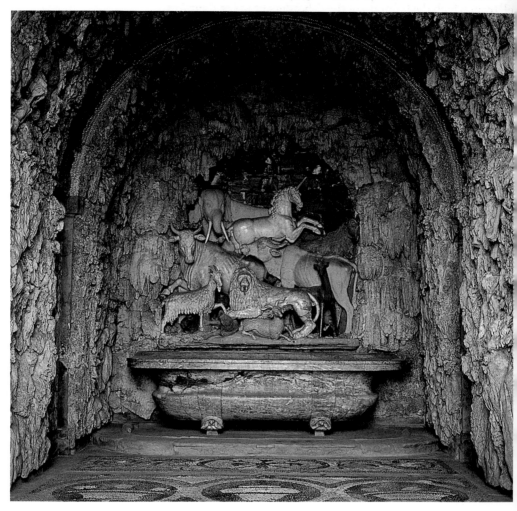

From the lemon garden the grotto is entered through a classical portal adorned with columns and pilaster strips, dating from the late 18th century. The grotto is composed of two chambers. The first is covered by a ceiling richly decorated with mascarons and festoons made of shells and marble tesserae. At the sides are two splendid marble basins decorated with marine animals and surmounted by groups of terrestrial animals that seem to emerge from the rock. The second chamber, smaller, has a barrel ceiling with incrustations of *pietra spugna* and a basin surmounted by a third group of animals dominated by the figure of a unicorn, a symbolic animal deemed to possess the power of purifying water, according to Greek mythology. This then was the message that the grotto was designed to express: purified water falls from the plaited hair of Fiorenza-Florence. Giambologna's bronze, placed inside the maze, symbolized the creation of a Medicean Garden of Eden. It should also be remembered that the originality of the composition, the precious materials and the striking impression they aroused in the past were surely intensified by the presence of water spouting from the floor and flowing copiously from the ceiling.

Many artists worked on the grotto, among them Tribolo and Giorgio Vasari, who may have modified Tribolo's project; Francesco Ubertini known as Bachiacca, probably responsible for the magnificent basins with festoons of fish and seashells; Bartolomeo Ammannati, who cast some of the animals in bronze in 1558; and Giambologna, who created the bronze animals now in the Bargello.

page 58). To the right of the grotto a stairway leads to the upper level, from which the fountain of the *Apennine* by Ammannati, dated 1563, can be admired. Lower down on the eastern side is an entrance leading to the little walled garden known as the *ortaccio*. This garden, echoing the tradition of the Renaissance herb garden, contains a recent collection of aromatic plants. Still on the eastern side is the *stufa dei mugherini*, the warm greenhouse planned by Cosimo III for the cultivation of the delicate Goa jasmine, known as 'the Grand Duke's jasmine' (*Jasminum Sambac*).

In recent years the garden has been enriched by a fine collection of azaleas, displayed at various points during the blossoming season. Standing against the walls enclosing the garden are espaliers of grape vines and fruit trees with borders of iris at their feet.

Another botanical curiosity is represented by some **dwarf pear** trees, at the center of the flowerbeds in the lower *parterre*, recalling the traditional form of Renaissance cultivation. In the flowerbeds peonies, spring bulbs and antique roses blossom splendidly in season.

To know more

C. Acidini, G. Galletti, *Le Ville e i Giardini di Petraia e Castello*, Pisa 1992.

G. and S. Tintori, *Gli agrumi ornamentali. Consigli dalla tradizione dei contadini giardinieri*, with an article by Paolo Galeotti. Bologna/Milan/Rome 2000.

Web: www.ambientefi.arti.beniculturali.it

Justus Utens,
Villa di Castello,
1599

The lunette by Justus Utens

In 1599, when Justus Utens depicted the villa, the garden had been completed. The painter's lunette gives a precise picture of the estate. Before the villa is the great lawn with fishponds; at the sides of the building, the flower gardens. The first fountain, with the statue of *Hercules strangling Antaeus* by Ammannati, is followed by the cypress maze; within it stands the statue of *Fiorenza* by Giambologna. Next comes the Grotto of the Animals, the *selvatico* and the bronze statue of the *Apennine*, also by Ammannati. On the right can be seen the *ortaccio* and the *ragnaia*; to the left and right of the central garden, extensive orchards.

The citrus trees

Citrus trees – lemons, oranges, citrons, bitter oranges – are distinguished by their upright stance and evergreen leaves. Their cultivation is closely linked to the myths handed down to humanistic culture from the Graeco-Roman world. According to mythology the Hesperides, the nymphs of the West, were the guardians of golden apples that grew in their garden. But the nymphs were unable to prevent Hercules from stealing the apples and taking them to Italy, where they flourished and spread. Citruses are also linked to the myth of eternal Springtime in the Garden of Eden. The plants flower and bear fruit at the same time, thus providing an excellent symbol of the continuity of life. Between the 16th and 17th centuries citrus trees became common in the villa gardens of Tuscany; having both practical and ornamental functions, they were used in cooking and in medicine.

The cultivation of citruses in Tuscany dates however from more ancient times. Lemon gardens are recorded as existing in Florence already in the Middle Ages, although the trees were at the time planted in the ground and covered with roofing in Winter.

Cultivation in urns became widespread in the 16th century, along with the custom of building *stanzoni*, or *limonaie*, where the trees were moved to protect them in cold weather. Citrus trees became such a characteristic element of the Tuscan garden that specific gardens or sections of gardens were designated to them. The lemon garden is often located in front of the *limonaia* or near it, as at Villa Gamberaia in Florence and Villa Marlia in the Lucchesia.

Citruses belong to the family of the *Rutaceae*. The most widely grown types are *Citrus*, to which belong lemons, oranges, citrons and grapefruit; *Fortunella*, to which belongs the kumquat; and *Poncirus*. The latter type has only one species, *Poncirus trifoliata*, a thorny orange used for hedges that are impenetrable to cats.

An extraordinary characteristic of citruses is the development of the varieties and the possibility of creating fruits of strange and monstrous shape, called 'teratological' which were particularly appreciated in the 17th century by the Grand Dukes and the Medici court Bartolomeo Bimbi depicted them in the late 17th century with 116 varieties and bizarre shapes, in a painting now in the Villa of Poggio a Caiano.

One of the most original varieties is the *Citrus aurantium* 'Bizzarria'. It has hybrid fruits, half orange and half citron colored yellow orange and green *Citrus aurantium* was discovered in Florence in 1644 in the garden of the Torre degli Agli.

In the Medicean gardens, Boboli and Castello in particular, enormous collections of citrus trees have been formed. In both gardens there are about one thousand potted citruses, all originating from plants in the ancient collection. This is a collection of priceless value, both botanical and artistic; many of the splendid urns are antique. In the garden of Castello the 'Bizzarria' is lovingly cultivated today by Paolo Galeotti, the gardener who must be hailed for having rediscovered and reproduced through grafting this unique, amazing variety.

Today lemon trees are grown in the Tuscan manner: in the classic 'free' form of a small tree; 'vase-shaped' (held open in the middle by means of props), or 'espaliered'. For their beauty and utility they have now returned to populate the finest gardens. Outstanding in this sense is the work of the Tintori family of Pescia. In their splendid nursery they have revived an art that seemed destined to disappear.

The statue of
the *Apennine*

Chronology

1537-1538 Cosimo I commissions Tribolo to design the garden.

1538-1548 Tribolo and Pierino da Vinci work on the fountains of *Fiorenza* and of *Hercules strangling Antaeus*.

1550 After the death of Tribolo, Davide Fortini becomes director of works; he is succeeded by Giorgio Vasari in 1554.

1560-1561 The *selvatico* or wilderness of ilexes and cypresses is planted around the basin with the bronze statue of the *Apennine* sculpted by Ammannati in 1563.

1588-1593 The garden is completed under Grand Duke Ferdinando. In 1599 it is painted by Justus Utens.

Second half of the 18th c. The *limonaia* is built to the west of the villa.

1785-1788 The fountain of *Fiorenza* is moved to the Petraia. Major changes are made in the layout of the garden.

Third decade of the 19th c. Joseph Frietsch, at the service of Ferdinando III di Lorena, transforms most of the vineyards and the *ragnaia* to the east of the villa into an English woods.

After 1918 Villa and garden, formerly Savoia property, pass to the Italian State. The villa houses the Accademia della Crusca while the garden is opened to the public.

Villa La Pietra

Restoration with invention

HOW TO ARRIVE

At the locality La Lastra
along the Via Bolognese.
Owner: La Pietra
Corporation S.A.
Address:
Via Bolognese 130
Bus: 25
tel.: +39 055 5007201
fax: +39 055 5007213
Visiting hours:
by appointment only

The great garden extending over a slope facing eastward was laid out starting in 1904 at the desire of the owner, Arthur Acton. The villa had been surrounded by a Baroque garden created by the Capponi family, of which only the lemon garden exists today, which was transformed into an English landscape garden in the 19th century.

In an isolated corner of the garden a stone inscription recalls the leading figures in the great work of transformation: the gardener designers Mariano Ambroziewicz, Pasquale Bonaiuti, Giuseppe Castellucci, Edwin Dodge and H.O. Watson. The list of outstanding figures in the interna-

of terraces are then placed *stanze di verzura*, garden rooms inspired by the Baroque gardening tradition. The garden rooms are furnished with architectural elements (largely salvaged from the past) and statues of Venetian provenance (many of them by Bonazza and Orazio Marinali).

Exedras, stone portals, pergolas, vases, balustrades, mascarons of various origin (many of the architectural elements are undoubtedly Tuscan) adorn the rich and varied garden, which remains one of the most striking testimonials to the vogue for antiquarian collections of the times. The preference for classical statues fits well with the strong, precise landscaping concept oriented toward revival of the Italian garden. Harold Acton recalls the creation of the garden in his book *Tuscan Villas*: "The decision to Tuscanize the so-called English garden was taken in 1904", writes

The garden looking
toward the *tempietto*

tional and local architecture of the times is long. The project, obviously, was grand in scope and did not derive merely from the initiative of an amateur.

The architectural layout reiterates the terraced system typical of the Tuscan garden. Within the system

Acton. "The garden looking to the south was demolished in the last century and restored by my father as he imagined it must have been".

Itinerary of visit

A great cypress avenue bordered in Bengali roses leads to the villa, a building complex of 15th century design transformed several times between the 16th and the 18th centuries. Before the house appear the first great topiaries in yew. Two curious cocks humorously exemplify the style, at once cultured and provincial, of the early 20th century designers.

Opening out to the left is the lemon garden with its magnificent *limonaia*, before which two *osmanto* in enormous vases catch the eye. Elements of great interest are the magnificent **walls decorated** in rustic style, presumably dating from the 18th century. At the center, around a little pool, great clipped hedges of box hold statues and stone benches.

Returning to the entrance to the villa, now the Florence branch of New York University, we enter the garden from the right. To the side of the building is a fine grotto decorated in a variety of materials. The formal gardens, now undergoing restoration, start in front of the building. Adorned with statues, the gardens offer magnificent views over Florence, looking southward. **A pergola** of Banksian roses, splendid in May, crosses the garden up to the great elliptical lawn sprinkled with volunteer thyme plants, at the southern boundary of the property. The path parallel to theater leads back to a lawn with a *tempietto*, from where it returns the level of the villa.

To know more
H. Acton, *Tuscan Villas*, London 1973 (It. trad. *Ville Toscane*, Milan 1973).
Web: villa.lapietra@nyu.florence.it

Detail of the lemon garden wall

Above
The lower garden with the great exedra

63

Villa Gamberaia

The garden of the Princess

HOW TO ARRIVE

Close to Settignano.
Owners:
The Zalum family
Address: Via del Rossel-
lino 72, Settignano
Bus: 10
tel.: +39 055 697205
fax: +39 055 697090
Visiting hours:
9:00 am - 6:00 pm
Admission: 10,00 €,
reduced 8,00 € for stu-
dents. From Nov. 1 to
March 1, visits only by
previous phone call or
e-mail. Accessible to the
disabled, Restrooms
Bookshop

Villa Gamberaia is one of the truly magic places in the world.
The splendid landscape, the views
of city and countryside, the architecture of the villa and the garden
are justly famous, making it one of
the most renowned gardens.
Not much is known of the first 15th
century building, consisting in all
probability of the small construction beside which the *limonaia* was
built later. The history of the gar-

ship several times until 1896, when
it was bought by Princess Ghyka.
It became the Princess' favorite residence, and she built a water
parterre as replacement for the 18th
century *parterre de broderie*. This
part of the garden has been com-
pletely transformed. An 18th century *cabreo* shows the Baroque
design of an elegant *parterre* that
ended in a *garenna*, or rabbit island.
The elliptical shape of the *garenna*
was reiterated in the belvedere of
cypresses and the semicircular
pool. The four sections of the
parterre were repeated, but with
the full and empty areas inverted
and flowerbeds turned into pools
of water. Borders of lavender, iris

The entrance avenue

den starts around 1610, when
Zanobi di Andrea Lapi had the villa built. The garden, which certainly already existed, was enlarged
in the 18th century when the property passed to the Capponi family, who owned it until 1854.
During the second half of the 19th
century the villa changed owner-

lilies, tree roses and oleanders were
reflected in pools lined by hedges
of box. Images of the garden in
flower, soon after its completion
have come down to us from
numerous photographers of the
early 20th century.
The central element of the garden
is a great grassy avenue, the bowl

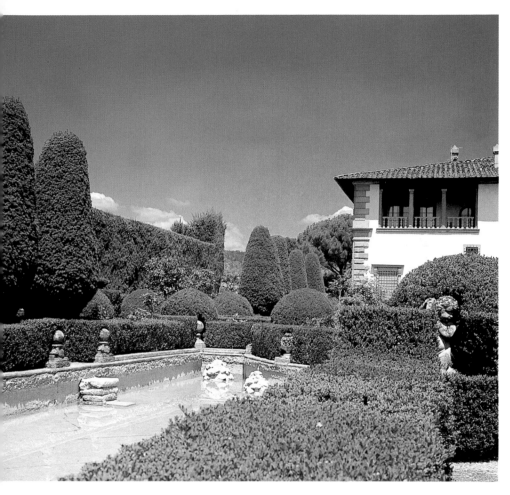

ng green. It forms a longitudinal axis of 225 meters that opens to the south onto the Arno Valley and ends to the north in a nymphaeum built into the hillside, surrounded by ancient cypresses. The transverse axis, about half as long, crosses the villa and forms the other main element of composition, the *gabinetto rustico*, with elliptical plan and walls decorated with shells and various materials. Through four asymmetrical stairways the *gabinetto* leads, on one side, to the first *selvatico* to the south, on the other to the lemon garden and the second *selvatico* to the north.

Itinerary of visit

From the exedra that forms the entrance on Via del Rossellino a gate opens onto the cypress avenue. The trees line both sides of the path like thick curtains. A visual corridor leads to the villa, which shows its northern side to the visitor. The main facade looks to the east, in the direction of Florence. The visitor's gaze is guided along the gently sloping avenue up to the house. Here there are no distracting elements and no visual opening onto the surrounding landscape or the garden. Arriving at the house we find, on the left, two arches that link the first floor

The modern *parterre*

65

to the chapel; on the right is a lawn. A great pine tree dominates and bounds the view over the valley. Passing under the side arcades of the villa we find the bowling green,

the axis that ideally and physically links the Arno River to the hill. This is not a rigidly symmetrical axis. One of the most distinctive features of the garden design is in fact its flexible architectural scheme, adapted with sensitivity to the logic of the place.

From here we follow a grassy path to enter the *gabinetto di roccaglia*, a striking architectural element that links the villa level with that of the *limonaia* and the two *selvatici*. In the shape of an elongated ellipse, it has walls richly decorated with niches and terra-cotta statues. From the back wall

The bowling green

The modern *parterre* in a photo from the early 20th century

The modern *parterre* as it appears today

Bowling green

Selvatico

Nymphaeum

Entrance avenue

emerge some figures, today partially destroyed. The *giochi d'acqua*, still existing, are controlled from a room under a stairway. Head-high jets of water were designed to drench visitors as they paused to admire the splendid, harmonious sandstone fountain.

On the right and left sides, two double ramps of stairs lead to one of the *selvatici* and to the *lemon garden*. The building on the right, its interior structured like a harmonious 15th century house, is in all probability the first core of the property owned by the Gamberelli family in the locality already

called *Gamberaia* in the 15th century (from the name of the pond for *gamberi*, or crayfish). In winter the great *limonaia* shelters the important collection of citrus trees, which are moved in spring to the ends of the four lawns. The *limonaia* garden, divided into four lawns, is embellished by a mixed border of perennials where arboreal peonies and Albertine roses flower

Limonaia

Gabinetto di roccaglia

Selvatico

Villa

Modern parterre

The tree roses
in flower

At right
Pelargoniums in
a terra-cotta urn

Next page
The exedra belvedere

in splendor. The *selvatico* of ancient ilexes, the ground below them carpeted with periwinkles, is linked again to the bowling green.

From the thick shade of the *selvatico* visitors thus pass, in an alternation filled with symbolic meaning, to the bright sunlight on the lawn.

From the lemon garden a path leads on to the *selvatico* to the south, where the *gabinetto di roccaglia*, the stone fountain and the fine pavement of colored pebbles can be seen from above. Through the *selvatico* we go to the water *parterre*, pausing below the majestic Corsican pine tree to enjoy a magnificent view over the Arno Valley.

We then go on to the water *parterre* created by Princess Ghyka. The arcade geometry of the cypress belvedere, where climbing roses are entwined high in the cypress branches, continues in the pattern of the hedges and the spherical shapes of the box bushes, while yew trees impose a vertical rhythm on the space enclosed by the *parterre*.

From here we can go on to the great lawn before the villa where a glimpse of Florence appears beyond the olive groves. Going around the building we return to the bowling green and continue in the direction of the **nymphaeum**. On the left the long construction houses the chapel and the ancient

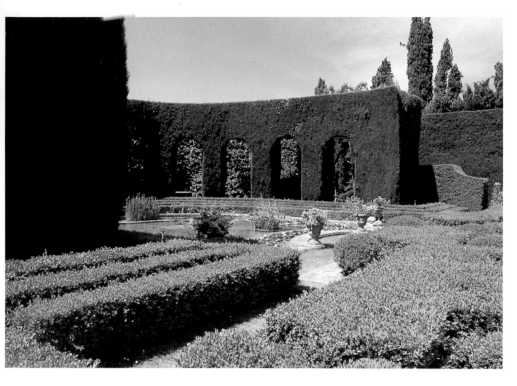

room where the game of *pallacorda* was played.

The nymphaeum, surrounded by cypresses, is preceded by a circular lawn surrounded by a wall, enclosing an area that is both majestic and intimate. It is a theater, probably designed for music and rendered enigmatic by the god emerging from the niche carved out of the hill (it may be Dionysus, as suggested by the shepherds and musicians appearing beside him). In April visitors can admire the splendid collection of **azaleas** blossoming along the leading to the villa.

To know more

M. Pozzana, *Una guida per conoscere Villa Gamberaia*, Florence 1998.

E-mail: villagam@tin.it

Web: www.villagamberaia.com

Chronology

1412 Documents record property owned by the Gamberelli family in the locality known as *Gamberaia*.

1610 Zanobi di Andrea Lapi purchases land at *Gamberaia*.

1717 After the death of Giovanni di Andrea Lapi the villa becomes the property of Vincenzio Maria and Piero Capponi. The Capponi family embellish the garden with new elements.

1854 Vincenzio Capponi sells La Gamberaia to Pietro Favreau. From this date up to the end of the century the property is sold several times.

1896 Catherine Jeanne Keshko, the Rumanian wife of Prince Eugenio Ghyka, buys the villa.

1910 Pietro Porcinai, the great Florentine landscape artist, is born in the vicinity of the villa. Martino, Pietro's father, works for Princess Ghyka as head gardener. With Luigi Messeri he creates the modern garden of Villa Gamberaia, so famous that

it soon becomes a model for numerous other gardens (for example, that of the castle of Ambleville in the Val d'Oise).

1924 Matilda Ledyard Cass, Baroness von Ketteler, purchases the villa.

1944 A German command in retreat sets fire to the building, used as cartographic center of the German Army. Garden and villa are severely damaged.

1952 The villa is donated by Matilda von Ketteler to the Holy See.

1954 Marcello Marchi buys the villa and carries out major restoration work. Since 1955 the garden, restored, is open to visitors.

1988 The villa passes to the Marchi heirs. It is inhabited by Nerina Von Erdber Krscenziewski, the Lithuanian wife of Marcello Marchi, until her death in 1990.

1995 The property is assigned to Luigi Zalum and his wife Franca Marchi.

Villa La Quiete

The refuge of the Palatine Electress

HOW TO ARRIVE

Between Serpiolle and Careggi. - Address: Via della Quiete ·14 Buses: 14, 20 tel.: +39 055 2757365/2757404 (the second number is that of the Florence Botanical Gardens, which manages the park). Visiting hours: by appointment only Free admission Guided visits. Accessible to the disabled

The complex is composed of the villa and a church built between 1686 and 1689 by Pier Francesco Silvani. The religious vocation of the site originated with the foundation of the Congregazione delle Minime Ancelle della SS. Trinità, which established here the Conservatorio delle Signore Montalve. It was then Anna Maria Luisa, the Palatine Electress and last member of the Medici family, who definitively transformed the place of her own spiritual refuge, inextricably mingling sacred and profane elements. Between 1724 and 1727 the villa-convent was thus adorned with a splendid garden designed by Pietro Giovannozzi in collaboration with Sebastiano Rapi, the Boboli gardener. Testifying to the deeply religious nature of Anna Maria Luisa is the fountain that decorates the outer walls, with the group of *Jesus Christ and the Samaritan Woman*.

Itinerary of visit

Although small in size the garden is extraordinarily interesting, conserving one of the very rare surviving *ragnaie*, woods for hunting considered a fundamental element in the creation of a garden for the nobility since the 15th century. The *ragnaia* of Villa La Quiete runs all along the eastern side of the garden and is formed of long parallelepipeds planted to ilex and bordered by high hedges of laurel and laurustine. Along these parallelepipeds, nets were once stretched to capture birds. Within the *ra-*

Above
View of the city

This page
The villa

Preceding page
The group of
*Jesus Christ and the
Samaritan Woman*

A tree-lined corridor
in the *ragnaia*

gnaia the **camere di verzura**, or garden rooms, with benches in stone or terra-cotta, are still well preserved. In summer this was a cool place in which to rest and listen to the birds singing. Here we can easily see how *ragnaie*, although designed for bird-catching, were also places of delightful repose. Below the terrace on which the villa faces is the lower garden, with an **orchard** bordered in box, vases and potted citrus trees (now undergoing restoration). On the left, through the encircling wall, we enter the *limonaia*. On the northern side an informal *boschetto* has been added.

71

Le Balze

A garden-terrace

HOW TO ARRIVE

In the immediate vicinity
of Fiesole.
Owner:
Georgetown University
Address:
Via Vecchia Fiesolana
26, Fiesole - Bus: 7
tel.: +39 055 59208
fax: +39 055 599584
Visiting hours: by
appointment only.
Information and reservations:
info@villalebalze.org
Partially accessible to
the disabled

This garden is one of the finest achievements of Cecil Pinsent (1884-1963), the refined English landscape artist who worked in Florence from the 1910s up to World War II. The breathtaking panorama and the ingenuity with which Pinsent exploited the possibilities of the site make this one of the most interesting initiatives in the trend toward revival of the formal garden.

Situated at the same height as Villa Medici on the southern slope of the Fiesole hill, the villa (now the headquarters of Georgetown University) and garden were constructed starting in 1914 by Pinsent and the historian of architecture Geoffrey Scott. The client, the American philosopher Charles Augustus Strong, commissioned Pinsent and Scott to direct the construction of the building and garden on a long, narrow terrace.

The theme, not an easy one, has been brilliantly developed in the overall composition, centered around the villa which opens at the sides onto the gardens laid out in a series of *stanze di verzura*, or garden rooms. On the south side a terrace that is splendidly panoramic although small in size overlooks the city. In the back, towards the

Upper right
The narrow terrace in
front of the villa

This page
One of the garden
rooms

The lemon garden

hillside, steps out leading to the upper terrace have been carved. A pergola ends in a broad sheltering roof. The most original feature of the garden is the **grotto** that opens below the ramp of stairs, in the finest tradition of the Italian Baroque garden.

The garden is entered from Via Vecchia Fiesolana. A *boschetto* of yew trees trimmed to shape forms a first garden room. Several of these 'rooms' are crossed to enter the **lemon garden**, divided into four sections and ornamented by a central pond. Two openings in the western wall lead to the terrace overlooking Florence, behind the house.

Continuing beyond the house we find a last garden room before a *boschetto* of ilexes distinguished by an unusual *romitorio*, or hermit's retreat. At the end of the garden, which drifts off into the countryside with borders of lavender and iris, stands the stone statue of a hermit.

To know more
M. Fantoni, H. Flores, J. Pfordresher, *Cecil Pinsent and his Gardens in Tuscany*, Florence 1995.

73

Podere Martello

The colors of a rural microcosm

visitor to wander slowly through the tall grass of the meadows dotted with olive trees and iris. A miniature **formal garden** is located in front of the house. A path across the field leads to the swimming pool through bluish-gray

HOW TO ARRIVE

Close to Maiano, along a panoramic road found just before arriving at Fiesole.
Privately owned.
Address: Via Benedetto da Maiano 22
Bus: 7
tel.: +39 055 613874
Visiting hours: by appointment only
Free admission
Guided visits
Accessible to the disabled

"We must speak of color in gardens; and it should be said immediately that in a garden, color rather than form is the great protagonist, the font of emotions, joy and ecstasy. Have you ever seen Boboli in Autumn? It is a prodigious symphony of bright or faded greens, of yellows, reds and browns; extending over a superb range of tones, with astonishing combinations and surprising contrasts".

Pietro Porcinai, speech given at the first conference of the Italian Institute of Color, 1957

The most significant and touching element of this extraordinary creation is perhaps its color: the visitor's eye is immediately struck by a symphony of azure, gray, silvery and yellow tones, especially in late spring.
Pietro Porcinai created this garden, his masterpiece, in the early 1970s. Around a country house, not particularly large but situated in a strategic position for its view over Florence, the expert landscape designer managed to create, with great ingenuity, a wholly natural landscape that interprets with extraordinary grace the spontaneous elements of the Tuscan farmland.
It is in fact a desire for harmony and beauty that seems to have suggested the choice of trees and flowers, as well as the connections between the areas in this rural microcosm where colors invite the

Daisies among the flagstones in the courtyard

Above
The little formal garden

hedges of *teucrium fruticans* and lavender.
An air of rural privacy is perfectly blended with the rationality that guides the layout of spaces and service facilities. An example of this is provided by the garage, located

underground, concealed by lavender, ivy and olive trees, and connected to the house by an underground passage.

The entrance from the street, with the great wooden door that recalls the traditional forms of rural archi-

lavender cotton alternate with vases of seasonal flowers. From here the path winds through the fields to the swimming pool, bordered by agapanthus and lavender cotton that light up the green of the hedge around it.

tecture, already announces the fascination of the place. It opens directly onto the paved courtyard, where clumps of daisies (*Bellis perennis*) emerge between the flagstones of Florentine sandstone. This detail alone, in its simplicity, expresses all of the poetic nature of the garden. And this rural, idyllic tone appears again in the little formal garden occupying a space in front of the house amid the olive trees, where silvery-gray clumps of

Further down is a white cottage vaguely reminiscent of the *Casa della Fata* in the Pinocchio park, also designed by Porcinai.

Surrounded by white lilies, roses and a pergola of grapevines, the cottage is linked to a tiny circular garden room ending in a steep rocky bank covered with St.-John's-wort. The steep bank is a modern interpretation of the sense of privacy afforded by the garden rooms of Baroque tradition.

Hedges of *teucrium* and *mahonia*

75

Villa I Tatti

A revival of the Italian garden

Laid out on the gentle slope of the Vincigliata hill, between Poggio Gherardo and Poggio al Vento, the garden was conceived as an outdoor extension of the house, a great *camera di verzura* to be discovered with delight upon entering the *limonaia*. Cecil Pinsent, the English architect and landscape design-

designed in the Italian style with the clear intention of revival, in the desire to re-establish the formal harmony attained by the gardens of the past, such as Villa Gamberaia. Pinsent declared his admiration for the art of the Italian garden, insisting that it was possible to learn to design a garden by taking as model those of the past.
Villa I Tatti is the manifest expression of this concept, shared by many intellectuals in the highly cultured and sophisticated British colony residing in the villas scattered over the hills around Florence at the turn of the century.

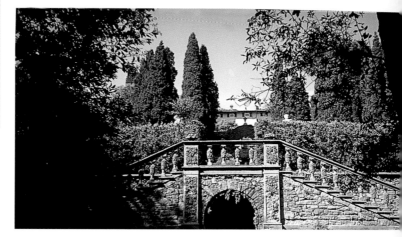

The lower grotto

er, had only recently come to Italy when Bernard Berenson, the renowned art historian and cosmopolitan, and his wife Mary commissioned him to direct the work of creating a garden on the property they were then restoring. The historian of architecture Geoffrey Scott was also involved in this initiative. The work, begun in 1911, concluded a few years later with the extraordinary reinvention of a Baroque garden skillfully structured as concerns spatial effects and based on the great formal suggestions of topiary art.
I Tatti is one of the first gardens

Itinerary of visit
On leaving the fine formal garden that stands before the villa and passing through the *limonaia*, the great **parterre**, so beautiful as to seem ancient, appears in all its splendor. Four terraced tiers slope gently downward, concluding in the last section where the central path, decorated with fine gravel patterns in homage to 17th century tradition, drifts off into a meadow.
Hedges of box design complex geometric motifs and a series of spires confers a marked rhythm on the high evergreen hedges. No con-

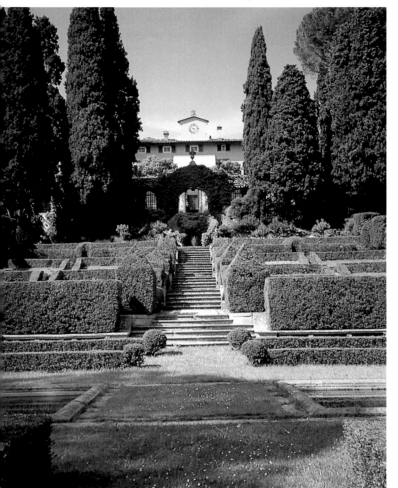

The garden seen
from below

Below
The avenue of cypresses

ble flight of stairs leads to the *sel-vatico* of ilexes planted geometrically according to the finest Renaissance tradition. Parallel to the garden, on the eastern side, a broad avenue leads to a rustic grotto.

:ession to color can be seen in a ;arden that deliberately empha-;izes the plastic and decorative ispects of plants clipped in topi-iry form.
\t the bottom of the terrace a dou-

To know more
M. Fantoni, H. Flores, J. Pfordresher,
Cecil Pinsent and his Gardens in Tuscany,
Florence 1995.
Web:www.vit.firenze.it
E-mail: info@tatti.it

Fonte Lucente

A garden lover's dream

"Many times I have been asked what is the secret of the beauty of my garden. I have answered that this garden reflects my life, with its joys, its grief, its loves and disappointments. The intense atmosphere breathed in the garden derives from the fact that all of my feelings, thoughts and doubts have remained here. Perhaps it has been the place of a particular concentration of interests, an environment that reflects my life".
Paolo Peyron

Situated on the slopes of the Fiesole hillside, the garden of Fonte Lucente is the creation of Paolo Peyron. Throughout his life he has designed, transformed, organized and adorned it with passionate enthusiasm and rare sensitivity.

Angelo Peyron purchased the villa in 1914 and commissioned the architect Ugo Giovannozzi (1876-1957) to transform the building in keeping with the eclectic style then in vogue.

Paolo Peyron inherited the property in 1919 and took residence there in 1934, beginning the work of creating a garden that has been developed since then, organically and consistently, almost without interruption.

Damage undergone in World War II called for reconstruction and work was intensified, giving rise to the **Italian garden**, the terraces the stairways, and the space for music dedicated to Riccardo Muti with a belvedere on the lake, beds of box, a pond, the woods adorned with antique garden architecture and numerous statues coming from the Veneto (about eighty in number, distributed throughout the garden and the woods).

At Fonte Lucente water is a fundamental element. There are 29 fountains built of elements of various provenance.

The **terraces** of the garden slope down along an ideal longitudinal axis, closed off by backdrops of tall cypresses in such a way as to offer a view of the city, which is seen as if through a telescopic lens (Paolo Peyron said that he created a stage with the city as backdrop)

Above
The pond

This page
The lower *parterre*

Preceding page
The garden near
the villa

A statue
in the woods

The garden
in front of the
chapel

The central path

On the eastern side of the property a pond has been built, on which faces the area dedicated to music. A visit to the villa in spring is recommended, to see the flowering of the **wisteria**, when the wall of the terrace in the first garden glows with a splendid indigo color.

80

Italian
garden

Central
walkway

Chapel

Area dedicated
to music

Pond

o know more
Romitti, *Il bosco di Fonte Lucente*, Flo-
ence 1997.

The garden seen
from below; in the
background,
the villa

81

Villa Medici

The invention of a landscape

HOW TO ARRIVE

In the immediate vicinity of Fiesole.
Privately owned.
Address:
Via Fra' Giovanni
Angelico 2, Fiesole
Bus: 7
fax: +39 055 2398994
Visiting hours: by
appointment only (for
groups on weekday
mornings in May)

Built on the side of the Fiesole hill turned toward Florence, at a point where the slope becomes steeper, Villa Medici dominates the landscape, the house admirably harmonizing with the surrounding terraces of its garden.

We owe this construction, certainly the most panoramic of the Medicean properties from the 15th century, to Giovanni di Cosimo de' Medici, fascinated by the stupendous view and by the modernity of this relationship with the landscape.

Giovanni, a highly cultured art lover and expert director of the Medicean bank, commissioned Michelozzo di Bartolomeo to build the villa. The garden was designed according to an innovative plan: a series of terraces reiterates the farming technique of cultivating

The lower terrace

terraced land, but transforms it into something noble and monumental. The villa co-exists with the garden that surrounds its two wings; one to the east, opening onto the terraced entrance level;

the other to the west, looking over a garden of smaller size.

We know that already in the 15th century citrus trees were cultivated here: bitter oranges grown on espaliers, for example, protected in winter by seasonal roofing, along with *incarnate* roses (*Rosa x alba incarnata*).

The garden is divided into two main terraced levels. A long avenue leads through the ilex woods to the first terrace on a level with the ground floor of the villa. To the left of the entrance is the late 18th century belvedere that dramatically frames an extraordinary view of the city. To the left can be seen the elegant *limonaia* dating from the same period.

The citrus urns are arranged around sectors of lawn bounded by stone curbs, dominated by two great paulownias (*Paulownia tomentosa*). To the right, on a slightly higher level, are climbing roses grown by the pegging down technique, in vogue during the second half of the 19th century (the rose shoots are fixed to pegs on chains).

Leaning against the right wall is a splendid *espalier* of bitter oranges recalling the important collection of citrus trees that was the pride of the garden in the 15th century. We know in fact that in 1455 *melaranci*, (*melangoli* or bitter oranges, *Citrus Aurantium* and *limoncelli*, *Citrus limon* 'Neapolitanum') were grown here. The long pergola flaming with Banksian roses, created in the early 20th century by Cecil Pinsent, leads to the lower terrace, divided into four beds: two consisting of lawns shaded by magnolia trees, the other two with box bushes. To the west of the villa is a little garden with box hedges, magnolias and a fine central fountain.

The garden in front of the villa

Chronology

1451-1457 Michelozzo di Bartolomeo, commissioned by Giovanni de' Medici, builds the villa.
1469 Lorenzo the Magnificent inherits the villa. Poliziano is a frequent guest and recalls the beauty of the place in his poetry, contributing to its mythical fame.
1492 An inventory compiled at the death of Lorenzo describes the garden: "...a garden behind said palace with several small orchards and fields walled and enclosed in masonry and a piece of land known as garden with cypresses and other trees forming a boschetto and a plot of vegetable garden".
1671 The villa is sold by Cosimo III to Vincenzo di Cosimo del Sera.
1772 Lady Orford becomes owner of the property. She commissions Niccolò Gaspero Paoletti to transform the villa. Paoletti creates a new carriage entrance, new grotesque-style decorations and a pavilion facing the villa. The work is completed in 1779.
1862 The new owner William Blundell Spence widens the entrance avenue and finds a section of Etruscan wall (as can be read in a stone inscription at the entrance).
1911 Lady Sybil Cutting, a friend of Bernard Berenson, asks Geoffrey Scott (who will become her husband) and Cecil Pinsent to direct the work of renovation. Pinsent creates a neo-15th century garden on the lower terrace, adding a long rose pergola, and transforms the garden on the west side by planting four magnolias.
1959 The villa is purchased by the Marchi Mazzini family.

To know more

Giardini medicei, edited by C. Acidini, Milan 1996.

I. Romitti, M. Zoppi, *Guida ai giardini di Fiesole*, Florence 2000.

Villa Corsi Salviati

A garden of statues and flowers

HOW TO ARRIVE

In the center of Sesto Fiorentino.
Owners: The Guicciardini Corsi Salviati family
Address: Via Gramsci 462, Sesto Fiorentino
fax: +39 055 2346863
Visiting hours: by appointment only

Detail of the encircling wall

Next page
Two views of the Baroque *parterre*

Villa Corsi Salviati, today the Florence headquarters of the University of Michigan, offers a very clear example of the changes made in a Tuscan garden over the course of its long history. A fine garden of statues, it has basins of water, fountains and beautifully decorated walls. Situated on the plain, it offers no memorable views of countryside or city, but is nonetheless splendid for the balanced linking of its spaces and carefully planned details.

The simple 16th century garden (appearing in a painting on the ground floor of the house) was enlarged in the 17th century with the addition of pools, statues, an orchard and a *selvatico*. In the 18th century the great *ragnaia*, over two hundred meters long, was planted and the vast Baroque-style parterre of flowers was constructed. Then at the beginning of this century the garden was restored again.

At the turn of the century English visitors were already struck by the beauty of a garden that, although dating from the Baroque period, was deemed to be of maximum interest. Great was their surprise on discovering, beyond the encircling wall that runs along today's Via Gramsci, a park abounding in statues, pools and walls decorated with *pietra spugna* and marble tesserae. The garden is composed of several different zones linked to one another. The visitor passes through a succession of 'rooms' with a growing sense of wonder. First comes the ornamental *par-*

terre with its precious flowerbeds bounded by hedges of dwarf box; then the lemon garden, today a simple lawn, in front of the *limonaia*; and lastly the English woods. Within the woods, at the beginning of the century, were created the fine *teatro di verzura*, or garden theater, and a maze of box.

Itinerary of visit

A secondary entrance leads to the garden theater with its backdrop of cypress trees dominated by the statue of *Apollo*. Around the theater grow centuries-old ilexes, which may have belonged to the villa's first *selvatico*. Half hidden by the trees is a little artificial lake with a cast iron bridge and a small **maze** of boxwood modeled after the one at Hampton Court. At the center of the garden is an of 18th century *parterre* of flowers with a complex

geometric design. The two great palm trees date from the 19th century restoration. From a rectangular basin adorned by statues of the four seasons at the corners leads a waterway that flows through the *ragnaia*. Beyond the circular basin with nymphs a wall with a fine wrought iron gate and statues on pilasters separates the *parterre* from the *limonaia* and its lawn. The *limonaia* has now become a theater. The facade of the villa extends to

Circular pond

Ragnaia

Limonaia

Parterre of flowerbeds

Garden theater

Maze

English woods

the west with two singular **aviaries**. The one on the right is today an open loggia with beautiful frescoed decorations.

To know more

G. Guicciardini Corsi Salviati, *La villa Corsi a Sesto*, Florence 1937.

The circular basin

A photograph from the second half of the 19th century which documents the changes in the garden

Chronology

1502 Simone di Jacopo Corsi buys the property from Luca di Andrea Carnesecchi.
1593-1603 Jacopo, Giulio and Bardo Corsi enlarge the building.
1632 Giovanni and Lorenzo di Jacopo Corsi undertake a second stage of work. Gherardo Silvani is probably responsible for the architectural part, while Baccio del Bianco, between 1640 and 1641, decorates some rooms with paintings that are now lost.
1644 A map documents the work on the garden, which appears divided into sec-

tors separated by walls: the flower garden, the *selvatico*, the orchard, a fishpond with exedra and a rabbit lawn.
1729 Antonio Corsi enlarges the villa and transforms the garden. The rectangular pool and the canal with thirteen little waterfalls are built.
1815 Amerigo Corsi begins transforming the eastern part of the garden into an English woods.
1866 Exotic plants are introduced.
1907 Giulio Giucciardini Corsi Salviati begins to restore the property.

Pratolino
The Villa Demidoff Park

HOW TO ARRIVE

In the immediate
vicinity of Pratolino.
Address: Via Fiorentina
276, Pratolino, Vaglia
Bus: 25A
tel.: +39 055 409155
Fax +39 055 409272
Visiting hours:
Apr.-Sept.:
Thursday-Sunday
10:00 am – 8:00 pm
March: holidays only
10:00 am – 6:00 pm
October: holidays only
10:00 am – 7:00 pm
Admission: 2,58 €,
reduced 1,55 € (6-14
years). Free admission
for under 6 and school
groups making
reservations by fax
Accessible to the
disabled
Restrooms
Café-restaurant
Bookshop

The avenue leading
from the entrance

Pratolino is today the most important landscape park in Tuscany. Its complex history spans immense changes in taste, fashions and trends in garden art. It is undoubtedly the most important example of transition from the late Renaissance garden to the modern English-style one. Its 19th century transformation resulted in virtually total destruction of the Late Renaissance park of Francesco I de' Medici, the model in its day for the most important European parks.

The Medicean park was famous for its grottoes, *giochi d'acqua* (waterworks) and the automata with their enigmatic meanings standing along the paths, probably created on the basis of alchemistic concepts. The basement of the Medicean villa held an amazing series of grottoes where visitors were struck by *giochi d'acqua*, automata and music. A great number of sculptures and architectural structures marked the stages of a journey through the 'park of the ancients' to the 'park of the moderns', located to the south, along a longitudinal axis that led from the avenue of spouting jets to the villa and then to the statue of the *Apennine*, the maze and the fountain of *Jove*.

The 16th century geometric structure was totally demolished by Ferdinando III di Lorena, who called upon Joseph Frietsch to redesign the park around 1818. The landscape artist produced a masterpiece at the price of drastic changes, creating a romantic park where a 16th century garden once lay. The broad, luminous landscape designed by Frietsch is unique in Tuscany, and great meadows, skillfully modeled, alternate today with thick woods of ancient oak trees.

Itinerary of visit

From the entrance on Via Bolognese an avenue lined with horse chestnuts leads to the buildings of the new farmhouse and stables. The main body, built by Buontalenti, was altered in the first half of the 19th century by the addition of the shorter wing of the building. From here we go on to the little lake before the statue of the *Apennine*, the world-famous sculpture by Giambologna with its *giochi d'acqua*. In summer the lake is covered with a lovely patchwork of water iris, lotus and water lilies. Behind the *Apennine*, through winding paths opening onto care-

fully modeled meadows, we go on to what was at the time of Francesco I the 'park of the ancients', arriving at the fountain of *Jove* to find what remains of the great *spugna*, now divided into two parts; the maze of laurel bushes was filled with *spugna*.

The fountain marked the northernmost part of the 16th century park, where a wall closed off the

The *Apennine* by Giambologna

The colossal statue-fountain, standing at the center of park, is its fulcrum and symbol. Created around 1580 by Giambologna, it represents an old man seated, leaning over the basin of water below in which his image is reflected.

Numerous jets of water, coming also from the head, transform the statue into a fountain. A submissive giant, man/mountain, man/river, the *Apennine* in its symbolic complexity, suggests a myriad of interpretations.

Originally, the giant contained several grottoes within it. Of these only one, carved out of the back of the colossus, still conserves part of the decorations in *pietra spugna* and calcareous concretions dating from the late 17th century restoration. The grotto below appears instead as a simple rustic grotto despoiled of all of its original decoration, but no less hauntingly evocative.

The *Apennine* was constructed by the technique of sculpture in masonry, with an iron framework and gravel underlayer covered in brick and plaster. At the foot of the statue is a semicircular basin. In the time of Ferdinando III it was transformed into a very natural looking pool.

Villa Demidoff

property. Now instead we can continue up to the Montili belvedere, with its splendid view over the valley toward Florence. Returning to the *Apennine*, in crossing the great meadow we reach the place where Buontalenti's villa once stood.

To the right a stone stairway leads up to a hexagonal-shaped chapel surrounded by a loggia, designed by Buontalenti and transformed during the course of the 19th century. Nearby is the tomb of Maria Demidoff.

Nothing remains today of the 16th century villa but the entrance

The Medicean aqueduct

Below the park of Francesco I a thick network of galleries and chambers for various mechanisms and for decanting water formed the arteries and veins of the garden, representing the peak of technical/hydraulic knowledge of the times. The whole array of marvels – fountains, grottoes with waterworks and automata – struck visitors to Pratolino with wonder, amazed at the ingenious blend of art and technology.

Other entrance

1 Entrance
2 Old post stage
3 Villetta
4 Buontalenti's chapel
5 Stables
6 Statue of the *Apennine*
7 Fountain of *Jove*

8 Villa
9 Great aviary
10 Statue of the *Mugnone*
11 Grotto of Cupid
12 Avenue of spouting jets
13 *Gamberaie*
14 Montili Belvedere

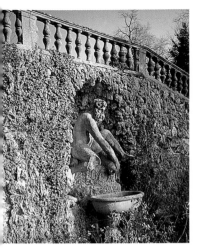

formed of two symmetrical ramps of stairs framing the fountain of the *Mugnone*.

At the sides, under the stairs, were once placed the first two grottoes: the grotto of *Fame*, with a peasant watering a dragon, and that of *Pan with the nymph Syringa*. The grottoes were famous for the automata moved by water-powered mechanisms.

Of the hydraulic and mechanical marvels there exist today only the statue of the *Mugnone* by Giambologna and the remains of the decoration at the entrance, redis-

The statue
of the *Mugnone*

The vegetation

In the 16th century the park covered nearly twenty hectares. It was surrounded by fields and farms worked by tenant farmers. Silver fir trees, once the distinctive feature of the park, formed an extensive woods in the northern part, around the statue of the *Apennine* and beyond. To the east the park was bounded by *ragnaie* composed mainly of ilexes. The maze was built of laurel.

Between the 18th and 19th centuries the vegetation of the park (enlarged to 160 hectares by the encapsulation of farmlands) underwent great change, finally assuming its present aspect, dominated by oaks introduced on a large scale. Among the varieties of oak present in the park the most majestic trees are to be found among the cerris, the English oak, the pubescent oak (all belonging to the genus *Quercus*).

Great trees in the park

covered by Princess Demidoff a few
years before World War II.
In front of the villa, and on the
same axis, begins the monumental avenue that ends in the **avenue
of jets**, another marvel of the park.
Before descending to the southern
part we can turn to the right to visit the villetta.
In front of the villetta is the grotto of *Cupid*, which once held a
gigantic statue of the demigod.
Returning along the axis of the villa we find what was once Buon-
alenti's great aviary. At left are five
pools of fresh water used for raising crayfish, the *gamberaie*, exten-
sively altered in the early 19th century. Before the *gamberaie* stood
the fountain of the *Springs*, a complex work designed by Ammannati.
Today only a few elements survive,
at the Bargello Museum.
Through the avenue of jets we
reach the bottom of the park,
beyond the 16th century boundary.
The fountain of the *Washwoman*
once stood in the 'park of the moderns'. Joseph Frietsch added a new
landscape park beyond the fountain. In doing so he exploited the
steep slope of the area and used

what remained at the time of the
agricultural structures once
belonging to the Medicean farm
surrounding the park, the flour mill
and the olive mill in particular.
Water became once more the cru-
cial element, with the landscape
artist laying out rock gardens,
waterfalls and *orridi* of great beauty (now not included in the visitors' itinerary).

To know more
*Pratolino Villa Demidoff Storia Arte Natu-
ra*, edited by Zeffiro Ciuffoletti, Florence
1990.

Justus Utens,
Parco di Pratolino (1599)

Chronology

1568 Francesco I de' Medici, the
alchemist prince, purchases
land at Pratolino.
1570-1575 Bernardo
Buontalenti, the favorite
architect of Francesco I,
designs the villa and starts
building it.
1579-1580 The park and farm
are created. The *Apennine* and
numerous other grottoes and
fountains are completed.
1587 Francesco I dies. Don
Antonio, his natural son, inherits the property, but it is Ferdinando I , Francesco's brother,
who continues the work.
Before 1710 The great maze in
the northern part of the park
and the artificial mountain

erected behind the *Apennine*
are demolished. In their place
Giovan Battista Foggini
creates the stone dragon.
1737 Pratolino slowly falls
into ruin, in a degradation
that continues up to 1814.
1773 Some statues are brought
to Boboli. The furnishings of the
villa are despoiled.
1814 Ferdinando III di Lorena
returns to Tuscany after the
Napoleonic domination and
commissions the landscape
artist Joseph Frietsch to
transform the park into a
modern English landscape
garden.
1821 The villa designed by
Buontalenti, now in a very poor

state of conservation, is
demolished.
1820 The architect Luigi de
Cambray Digny creates the
Montili belvedere, an elegant
neo-classical pavilion.
1845 The park becomes
the personal property of the
Grand Duke, remaining so even
after the Lorraines abandon
Tuscany in 1859.
1872 Pratolino is sold to Prince
Paolo Demidoff.
1969 After the death of the
last Princess Maria Demidoff,
the estate is sold at auction.
1981 The Province
of Florence buys the park of
Pratolino and opens it to the
public.

Villa di Bellosguardo

The garden of the opera singer Caruso

HOW TO ARRIVE

West of Florence, near
Ponte a Signa.
Address: Via di Bellos-
guardo 54, Lastra a
Signa - Bus: Lazzi from
Piazza Adua
tel.: +39 055 8721783
fax: +39 055 8722230
Visiting hours
in summer:
Saturday 2:30-7:00 pm
Sunday 9:00-12:00 am,
2:00-7:00 pm.
in winter:
Saturday 3:00-6:30 pm
Sunday 9:00-12:00 am,
3:00-6:30 pm
Free admission
Guided visits by
appointment only, also
in the closing days.
Accessible to the dis-
abled - Restrooms

Over the curves of the winding country road that leads from Ponte a Signa to Malmantile, through cultivated fields, olive groves and woods, we arrive at the Villa di Bellosguardo.

Situated southeast of Ponte a Signa, the villa lies at the center of a park atop the hill known as Colle Alberti. Seen from above, the estate is the dominating feature of the surrounding landscape, its lozenge shape standing out clearly from the geometric pattern of the fields around it. Behind two gates opening onto the road, the main one to the north, the service entrance to the south, appears the splendid

around 1915 by the architect Sabatini for one of the villa's last owners, the tenor Enrico Caruso. Enclosed between the two buildings and the portico are geometric parterres of box, with the collection of potted citrus trees.

The garden is distinguished by a rhomboid design that fits majestically into the landscape. A system of perspective **views** harmoniously links the park to its surrounding countryside (a clear perception of the original design is now unfortunately hindered by the fencing added by Caruso).

The garden is entered through the southern gate, the second one for visitors coming from Ponte a Signa. Passing beside the custodian's house, built by Caruso, we arrive at a broader tree-lined space inviting the visitor to pause to admire the scenery. The central path, the only one that slopes gently uphill, leads to the forecourt of

A corner of the park with the column erected upon completion of the work ordered by Enrico Caruso

wooded backdrop of the *selvatico*. The layout of the garden dates from the last twenty years of the 17th century and was probably designed by Giuliano Ciaccheri for Orazio Ruberto Pucci. Today the villa consists of two symmetrical bodies joined by a portico, built

the villa between thick curtains of ilex, laurel and viburnum.

The two main bodies of the building are famed by wide lawns, bordered in box. The one on the right was originally the old *casino di delizia*, probably built in the late 16th century by Abbey Alessandro

Pucci (thought to be designed by Giovanni Antonio Dosio). On the side of the building, near a well, a stone inscription in Latin along with its translation exhorts the guest to indulge in meditation. The second building, originally great octagonal basin. With the two buildings now behind us, we cross the lawn to enter the *selvatico*. Before us are magnificent **tiers of stone** and another spectacular view. Two statues of women symbolizing *Spring* and *Summer* mark

The formal garden

small in size and destined to be used for storing grain, was enlarged over the years, reaching its present size at the time of Caruso. Through the portal that opens in the wall between the two buildings, adorned by vases and benches, we cross the portico and go down to the formal garden, distinguished by *parterres* of box and citrus trees in terra-cotta urns. Beyond a lawn slopes gently downward, inviting us to discover another part of the garden, built in tiered terraces.

A splendid stone **stairway**, of unusual polygonal shape, leads to the second level of the garden. The composition is completed by a pool of water shaded by a majestic linden tree. A double ramp of stairs completes the layout of garden toward the countryside. The path leads back to the villa skirting a three avenues. The central one leads to the Zitti belvedere, opening onto the valley below, in the direction of Florence. This place is consecrated to silence and contemplation, and its name, which means "hush" or "quiet", derives from the attitude of the mysterious stone figures who seem to observe the visitor. Lastly, a column expresses the gratitude of the workers employed by Caruso in reconstructing the park.

To know more

F. Borghini, *La Toscana di Caruso*, Florence 1998.
S. Bonavoglia, F. Parrini, *Mecenati e artisti in villa. Un patrimonio nascosto*, Lastra a Signa/Campi Bisenzio 1999.
E-mail: villacaruso@tin.it
Web: www.villacaruso.it

95

Poggio a Caiano
The garden of Lorenzo the Magnificent

HOW TO ARRIVE

In the center of Poggio a Caiano.
Address: Piazza de' Medici 14
tel.: +39 055 877012/ 8798432
Visiting hours:
until Oct. 27, 8:15 am-5:30 pm; Nov.-Feb.: 9:00 am-3,30 pm.
Closed May 1, Christmas and New Years Day
Admission: 2,00 €
Free admission for under 18 and over 65
Guided visits every hour
Accessible to the disabled - Restrooms

Encapsulated today by the town of Poggio a Caiano, the villa was built in a slightly elevated position. The effect is heightened by the solemnity of the building with its bastioned wall recalling the fortified architecture of the past. It was just this singular encircling wall that once enclosed a part of the 16th century garden now lost.

The villa of Lorenzo the Magnificent was begun in 1485 to the project of Giuliano da Sangallo, but was still unfinished in 1492, the year of Lorenzo's death. In all probability no garden existed until the middle of the 16th century, when Cosimo I commissioned Tribolo and Davide Fortini, his son-in-law, to lay out the surrounding area. A lunette by Justus Utens shows how the garden was divided into sections planted to dwarf fruit trees. On the eastern side, beyond the wall, was created a garden very similar in structure to that of numerous other Medicean gardens, divided by four crossing avenues and centered around the *boschetto* for bird-catching. Of this garden, transformed between 1819 and 1830 by Pasquale Poccianti, no trace remains today. Poccianti also built the *limonaia* and the cistern to collect water.

Entering from Via Pistoiese we cross the first garden with flowerbeds of curvaceous shape and great cedar trees. From here there is a fine view of the villa embellished by its Della Robbian frieze. Many scholars believe it to be symbolically linked to the agricultural activity undertaken

Le Cascine di Tavola

Not far from the Villa di Poggio a Caiano it is possible to visit (from the outside) the agricultural core of Lorenzo's property, the farm called Cascine di Tavola, a quadrangular building with four towers at the corners. The complex was conceived in the 1470s as an experimental farm for raising cattle, producing cheese and planting various crops, such as rice. The land was reclaimed and the waters of the Ombrone river channeled to resolve the problem of continuous floods.

Of the extensive transformation carried out in the 15th century, traces remain today in the surrounding landscape. The broad straight tree-lined avenues still provide a pleasant place to walk.

by Lorenzo at Poggio a Caiano. To the right of the villa a stairway leads to the garden closed off on the southern side by Poccianti's huge *limonaia*. This garden, of very elegant form, has recently been embellished by flowers reviving the 19th century taste for color.

Continuing along the west side of the *limonaia* or returning to the level of the villa and descending the stairs behind it, we reach the 19th century *boschetto* with interesting trees.

To know more

M. Pozzana, *Il paesaggio, le ville, i giardini*, in "Antiche terre di Prato. Una nuova Provincia", Florence 1994, pp. 11-43.
Giardini Medicei, edited by C. Acidini, Milan 1996.

The villa

Preceding page
The side garden

Other gardens in Florence and around it

Giardino dell'Iris
Piazzale Michelangelo
Visiting hours: open from May 2 to 20, 10:00 – 12:00 am, 3:00 – 7:00 pm.
Free admission
tel.: +39 055 483112
(Italian Society of Iris)
The garden was created as site for the international iris show/competition held each year in spring. A visit during the flowering season (April-May) is particularly interesting.

Giardino dell'Orticoltura
Via Bolognese 17
Visiting hours: 8:00 am – 6:00 pm
(seasonal variations) Free admission
tel.: +39 055 483698
Created by the Tuscan Horticultural Society in the mid-nineteenth century, the garden is embellished by the iron and glass greenhouse designed by Giacomo Roster, built in 1880. It has been a public garden since 1930.

The garden of Villa Schifanoia

I Collazzi
Via Volterrana 7, Scandicci, Florence
Privately owned. Visits are not allowed.
The villa, attributed to Michelangelo, is preceded by a cypress avenue and surrounded by terraced gardens (the lower portion is a lemon garden).
The swimming pool is by Pietro Porcinai (1939).

Palazzo Medici Riccardi
Via Cavour 1
Visiting hours:
9:00 am – 7:00 pm
closed on Wednesday
Admission: 4,00 €,
reduced 2,50 €
tel.: + 39 055 2760340
Created around the middle of the 15th century, the garden appears profoundly changed today. In the first two decades of the 20th century Enrico Lusini, commissioned by Arturo Linaker to redesign the garden, eclectically combined 15th century and Baroque elements.

Palazzo Vivarelli Colonna
Via Ghibellina 28
Open during exhibitions only
tel.: +39 055 2625955
Recently restored and open only in particular circumstances, the garden is divided into geometric beds planted to box and has a *boschetto* of camellias on the eastern side. At the back of the garden is an 18th century wall-fountain.

Parco delle Cascine
From Piazza Vittorio Veneto to the Indiano Viaduct.
Always open.
The park was given its definitive layout in the late 18th century. Interesting features designed by Giuseppe Manetti: the icehouse/pyramid and the two *tempietti*. At the western end, in 1865, the monument to an Indian prince was built.

Parco del Neto
Via Vittorio Emanuele, Calenzano
Visiting hours: winter 8:00 am – 5:00 pm, closed on Monday;
summer 8:00 am – 8:00 pm
tel.: +39 055 8874515
Fine examples of *taxodium* border the 19th century pond. The park originally belonged to Villa Gamba al Neto. Open to the public, it is now owned by the Municipality of Calenzano.

Parco delle Cascine,
ice-house/pyramid

Below
The great horse chestnut
at Villa I Collazzi

Parco Strozzi al Boschetto
Via di Soffiano 11
Seasonal visiting hours
Tel.: +39 055 2767120 / 2767127

Park restored by Giuseppe Poggi around
the middle of the 19th century. Interesting
structures in Egyptian style.

Villa di Careggi
Viale Gaetano Pieraccini 17
Visiting hours:
Monday – Friday, 9:00 am – 6:00 pm
Saturday 9:00 am – 1:00 pm
Tel.: +39 055 4279755

Medicean villa associated with Lorenzo
the Magnificent. The original design of
the garden can hardly be distinguished
today due to the trees planted at later
times. The *limonaia* and the grotto below
the villa are interesting.

Villa Corsini a Castello
Via della Petraia 38
Seasonal visiting hours by appointment only
Free admission
Tel.: +39 055 450752

The villa has a monumental Baroque
facade. Passed from the Rinieri to the
Corsini family in the late 17th century, it
was transformed by Antonio Maria Ferri,
who created the garden of the Four Seasons and a French garden.

Villa Schifanoia
Via Boccaccio 121
Visiting hours: by appointment only
Tel.: +39 055 46851

Italian garden commissioned by Myron

Taylor in the 1930s; beautiful *parterre*.
The villa is the site of the European University.

Villa Stibbert
Via Stibbert 26
Visiting hours: summer 8:00 am – 7:00 pm,
winter 8:00 am – 5:00 pm
closed each Thursday morning
Free admission - tel.: +39 055 475520
The museum has different visiting hours from
the park

Park created in the second half of the 19th
century by Gerolamo Passeri and Giuseppe
Poggi for Frederick
Stibbert. At the center
of the pond is an
Egyptian-style *tempi-
etto*; beyond, a *limon-
aia*. The villa, now a
museum, houses the
collections of its for-
mer owner.

Villa Il Ventaglio
Via Aldini 12
Visiting hours: 9:00 am
– 5:30 pm
(seasonal variations).
Free admission
tel.: + 39 055 5802837
The park was created
in the mid-19th centu-
ry by Giuseppe Poggi.
Important trees and
broad lawns traversed
by a carriage drive
leading to the villa.

MAR LIGURE

MAR TIRRENO

Corsica
(Francia)

Canale di Corsica

Arcipelago Toscano

I. di Gorgona
(Livorno)

I. di Capraia
(Livorno)
Capraia
447

Can. di Piombino

Can. di Piombino

I. Pianosa
(Livorno)

Marciana Marina
Portoferraio
▲1018
M. Capanne
I. d'Elba
(Livorno)

Porto Azzurro

Parco Nazionale
d. Arcipelago Toscano

Formiche
di Grosseto

I. del Giglio
(Grosseto)

Porto S. Stefano
635 ▲ Cosa/A
M. Argentario

Pietrasanta
Bagni di Lucca
Barberino
di Mugello
A1 ❸
❸❼
S.S.325
le Pizzorne
1026
Forte dei
Marmi
Camaiore
Marlia
Collodi
❹ ❺ Pescia
Pistoia
Santomato
❺❶
❺❸ Prato
Biviglia
Viareggio
❶⓿
❶❸
❶❹
❶❶ ❶❷
Capannori
Montecatini
Terme
A11
Campi
Bisenzio
Signa
Sesto Fio
Fi
Lucca
❹❶
❹❹ ❶❻
❶❺
Empoli
❾
❼
FIR
S. Giuliano Terme
❹❺
❺❷ 917 ▲
❹❻
Pisa
M. Pisano
Fucecchio
Scandicci
Im
Arno
❹❷ 4
Cascina
S. Croce
sull'Arno
S. Miniato
❸❽
❹⓿
S. Ca
in Val
Marina di Pisa
Tirrenia
Pontedera
S.G.C. FI-PI-LI
Ponsacco
❺⓿
Collesalvetti
Casciana
Terme
Castelfiorentino
❽
Certaldo
Castellina
in Chianti
Livorno
A12
Rosignano
Marittimo
S. Gimignano
Poggibo
S.S.429
Castiglioncello
674
M. Vitalba
T O S C A N
❸
Rosignano
Solvay
Volterra
Colle
di Val d'Elsa
Mont
Cecina
Cecina
❷❷
Sovicille
Sien
Marina
di Cecina
619 ▲
Pomarance
❸❺
❷⓿
Larderello
Colline Metallifere
Castagneto
Carducci
1060
le Cornate
Monticiano
San Vincenzo
Campiglia
Marittima
Massa
Marittima
Cornia
Roccastrada
❶❾
Piombino
S.S.1 AURELIA
M. Leon
614
Follonica
Gavorrano
G. di
Follonica
Vetulonia
Montepescali
Punta Ala
Punta Ala
630 ▲
Poggio Ballone
Castiglione
della Pescaia
Grosseto
10
Ombro
Marina
di Grosseto
Scansa
Talamone
S.S.1

1: 1 100 000
0   10 km
Cartografia LEGENDA

100

In Tuscany

Villa di Bivigliano

A 17ᵗʰ century woods

HOW TO ARRIVE

Near Bivigliano,
reached by a brief
detour from
Via Bolognese.
Owners:
The Pozzolini family
Address: Via del Viliani
84,
Bivigliano, Florence
Bus: SITA
tel.: +39 055 4067717
fax: + 39 055 406326
Visiting hours: in the
daytime, all year long.
Admission:
6,00 €
Guided visits: by
appointment only for
groups of at least 8
persons with two weeks
advance notice. For
groups of at least 8
persons and with two
weeks advance notice,
luncheons, dinners,
and ceremonies are
organized.
Partially accessible to
the disabled
Restrooms

A broad lawn flanked by cypresses stands before this beautiful villa, of Buontalenti influence. To its left is the elegant chapel dedicated to the Madonna of the Snow. The building, with a formal terraced garden, was constructed in the early 17ᵗʰ century by the Ginori family. The most fascinating element of the estate is the great woods extending for over 12 hectares. Created in the 17ᵗʰ century, it was transformed by the Pozzolini family, who became its owners around the middle of the 19ᵗʰ century.

On the left of the building we enter the formal garden. Composed of two terraces, it is situated to the south, facing on the valley that overlooks Florence. The gaze sweeps over an enormous landscape, bounded on the right by the monumental cypress avenue.

The first level of the garden consists of four beds of box with a lovely fountain in the center. The second level is an exquisite **orchard**, recalling the 16ᵗʰ century tradition of orchards in the Medicean gardens. Below appears a modern pergola.

The natural scenery surrounding the garden is the wooded, mountainous one of the Mugello, and it may have been the local features of the landscape to suggest the creation of the woods, a real hunting park planted at the wish of Filippo Ginori near the end of the 17ᵗʰ

The grotto in the park

The cypress avenue

Below
The fountain in the formal garden

century (1690). The woods, situated beyond the access road, are traversed by a broad, straight avenue that slopes gently down to a rustic **grotto** built of stone.
The grotto, surmounted by a terrace with balustrade, is reached by an inner winding staircase (an inscription on the right records the year it was built: 1690). Before the grotto a vast circular space, surrounded by majestic trees, calls to mind other theatrical areas in the garden.
During the 19th century the woods was enriched by an interesting collection of conifer trees, including over one hundred examples of sequoia and tuje which have found an ideal environment in the damp climate of the Mugello.

Castello del Trebbio

The origins of the villa garden

HOW TO ARRIVE

North of Florence,
in the vicinity of San
Piero a Sieve.
Owner:
Lorenzo Scaretti
Address:
Via del Trebbio 1,
San Piero a Sieve,
Florence
tel. and fax: +39 055
8456230 - E-mail:
tea@terraditoscana.com
Visiting hours:
by appointment
only for groups
of at least 20
persons (max 30).
Admission: 10,50 €,
guided visit included
Poorly accessible to
the disabled
Bookshop

The grapevine
pergola

A typical Medieval construction built on the crown of a hill, the Castello del Trebbio offers a splendid view over the Mugello landscape. Transformed into a modern residence by Michelozzo di Bartolomeo around the middle of the 15th century, the castle has never entirely lost its original aspect of fortress. It boasts an extraordinary garden, a rare example of *hortus conclusus* preserved intact over the centuries and still today recognizable in its main elements.

This is the history of the castle. Giovanni di Bicci came into possession of Trebbio in 1386. After Giovanni's death in 1428, his property passed to Cosimo and Lorenzo; and already in 1428 Cosimo began to invest in the Mugello region. This policy was pursued more energetically starting from 1434, the year when the Medici's exile was revoked and they were called back to the city. It thus seems probable that it was Cosimo himself who commissioned Michelozzo to renovate the castle. In 1451 Trebbio passed to the secondary branch of the Medici family. Lastly, in 1936, it was inherited by the Scaretti family through a complex series of transitions. And it was with Marjorie Jebb Scaretti that the final transformation of the house and garden took place.

The finest feature of the garden is its splendid **pergola**, repeatedly imitated and reiterated in the construction of 20th century gardens. It has 46 columns of Michelozzian influence built of brick with sandstone capitals either *a foglie d'acqua semplice* or with fluting. Sixty-nine grapevines (*Vitis vinifera*) climb up the columns to form a green, living roof.

The architectural features that distinguish the Michelozzian garden appear remarkably innovative. Almost prefiguring the plan that was to become characteristic of the villa garden, one of the first gardens conceived to ornament a castle was created. On the right side of the castle is the orchard, structured in three terraces. The first terrace is entirely occupied by the pergola while the second is instead a real orchard. The second terrace originally held another pergola, now lost. The use of terraces in laying out the garden recalls the farm terracing used to cultivate steep hilly lands, a custom that was molding the Tuscan agricultural landscape already by the 14th century and that became widespread in the 16th century.

In front of the house, where the lawn with the 'green pavilion' represented in a lunette by Justus Utens (1599) is located, Marjorie Jebb Scaretti has designed a simple formal garden with sections planted to box and roses. On the right appears a rock garden of typically English taste, adjacent to the wall of the house; further to the right is a grove of fruit trees. At the back, sheltered by a backdrop of cypress trees, is a lawn and an area set aside for outdoor games. Lady Scaretti, in collaboration with her son Lorenzo, has supplemented the cypresses that surround the house, planted by the Philippine Fathers in 1820 and by Austrian prisoners of war lodged in the castle in 1917. In the area of the pergola and the lower terrace the 20th century alterations were more limited, consisting only of the creation of a double hedge of cypress with borders of roses and

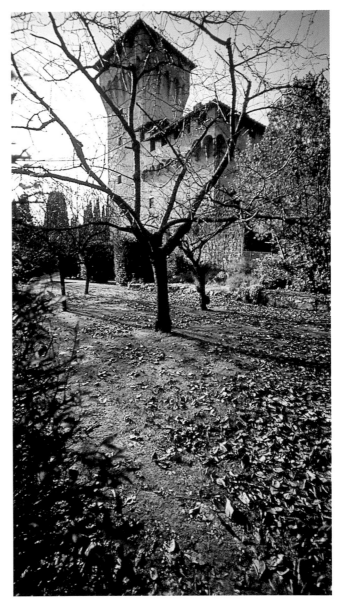

lavender. The pergola has remained unchanged and the orchard still has the pool and the sections planted to *erbaggi*, or herbs, appearing in the lunette by Utens.

The garden near the castle

To know more
Giardini Medicei, edited by C. Acidini, Milan 1996.
Web: www.y-knot.net

Castello di Barberino di Mugello

An open-air theater

The wisteria pergola

From the center of Barberino di Mugello the castle and its garden are not visible today, since thick vegetation conceals the construction in spite of its dominating position. The Medieval castle, built by the Cattani family around the year One Thousand, remained their property for many centuries. It was transformed into a manor house in the 15th century, when its military and defensive functions had become obsolete.

After the castle had passed from Leopoldo Cattani to the Manelli Galilei Riccardi family, in 1915, it was bought by Luigi Dapples, who transformed the villa and embellished it with a large garden, commissioning the project of the architect Agenore Socini.

Laying out the hillside in front of the castle could not have been an easy task for Socini, considering its steep slope (almost 25 meters difference in altitude). The problem was resolved by creating a system of terraces buttressed by traditional stone walls. In 1924 Giulio Coronati, in describing the garden "in 15th century style", found it "abounding in laurel, cypress, myrtle and other evergreens, with pergolas of roses of every variety and splendidly flowering espaliers". The visitors' admiration shows how Socini's garden represents a highly successful revival of the 15th century Tuscan garden.

The layout of the garden presents very particular features, appearing as an enormous triangle, the tip turned toward the town and the base toward the castle. The eastern side bounded by a monumental cypress avenue and a pergola, the western side by another pergola and the woods. The garden is thus distinguished by two very long pergolas, originally of roses, later of grapevines and now of wisteria.

Three distinct parts can be observed. Below the castle is the 'garden theater', followed by garden rooms of box with cypress and ilex trees, and last an orchard and a vegetable garden between the two pergolas. The various parts are arranged hierarchically according to a canon theorized and applied

already in the 16th century (a canon which, in later times, was always observed in designing formal gardens). The ornamental garden is placed close to the building while the orchard and the other productive parts follow and are connected to the *selvatico*, to the *ragnaia* for bird-catching and to the farm landscape.

The **ornamental garden** is interpreted as a black-and-white garden, that is, without flowers, rhythmically marked only by the compact volume of the hedges and the vertical soaring of cypress and ilex. The central sector, containing a pool of water, is composed of four sections of box with cypress trees and small statues.

Itinerary of visit

Descending from the castle, we find on the right the *teatro di verzura*, or garden theater, situated at the center of a group of tall trees in homage to the traditional Italian garden. Four tiers of turf, marked off by spheres of box, form benches for the spectators. The rec-

crenellations. The complexity of the garden's geometric design and the harmonious linking of the parts reveal the great ingenuity of its designer, and even suggest the possibility that Socini may have received help from another, perhaps a foreign landscape artist.

Returning to the courtyard of the

tangular stage is enclosed by a hedge of laurel surrounded by cypresses.

In the lower part of the garden is the orchard, divided into six sectors. Numerous fruit trees grow here, apples, pears, plums and apricots in particular. From the orchard there is a fine view of the imposing castle with its towers and

castle we find a small rose garden, closed off by a pergola. A central bed of sinuous profile frames two monumental cedars.

Adjacent to the castle is a large park. It may have been Luigi Dapples himself, together with his brother, who decided to plant numerous conifers. In the vicinity of the garden theater in particular grow fine examples of *Sequoia sempervirens*, *Abies alba*, *Abies pinsapo*, and *Cedrus atalantica* var. *glauca*.

To know more

M. Pozzana, S. Salomone,
Il castello di Barberino di Mugello, Florence 1999.

The formal garden

At left
A statue
in the garden

Parco di Pinocchio

A fairy-tale told by nature

HOW TO ARRIVE

Not far from Pescia,
take the Chiesina
Uzzanese exit from
highway A11 (Firenze-
Mare).
Owner: Fondazione
Nazionale Carlo Collodi
Address: Via San Gen-
naro, Collodi, Pistoia
Bus: *Lazzi*
tel: +39 0572
429342/429613
www.pinocchio.it
e-mail:
pinocchio@pinocchio.it
Visiting hours: every day
all year round from
8:30 am to sunset.
Guided visits (tel.: +39
0583 978205)
Admission: 7,00 €;
reduced 5,00 € (under
14 and over 65);
5,00 € for groups;
reduced 3,00 €
Free admission for
under 3
Partially accessible to
the disabled
Restrooms
Bookshop

The Pinocchio Park is the only example in Italy of an art park created to illustrate a fairy tale, with a natural itinerary marked by the sculptures of contemporary artists.

The construction of the park, linked to the name of Rolando Anzilotti, took place in two successive stages and involved different artists.

First to be built was the area where the *Red Shrimp Tavern* and the *Laboratory of Words and Figures* are found today.

Then the *Land of Toys* was completed, designed as a garden itinerary along which statues are placed to illustrate the major episodes in the story of Pinocchio. Nature, ingeniously modeled by the landscape artist Pietro Porcinai, thus fully participates in the adventurous life of Collodi's marionette.

Contrasting with the elegant simplicity of the first portion of the park, inaugurated in 1956, is the elaborate modulation of the land distinctive of the second part, rich in botanical varieties, inaugurated in 1972; covering a little over one hectare, it has been conceived as a space divided into two sections bounded by a great avenue of ilexes. Three artificial hillocks create the illusion of a space larger than it really is.

Itinerary of visit

The entrance to the garden is located beside the *Red Shrimp Tavern*. After crossing the lawn with the statue of the *Good Fairy, Pinocchio and the Dove* by Emilio Greco, we find on the right a little square laid out like a checkerboard and the building of the *Laboratory*; in front of it, a woods of tall ilexes trimmed in geometric shapes encloses the *Piazzetta of mosaics* by Venturino Venturi. Within the woods is a playground for children and a number of resting places with wooden benches and tables. At the end of the woods a paved path leads to the *Land of toys* (Paese dei balocchi).

The whale
in the Collodi Park

We then enter Pinocchio's *Village* with the imposing figure of the *Carabiniere* by Pietro Consagra standing ready to bar the way. Continuing along the path, built of stones from the ancient streets of Pescia, we climb the first of the three artificial hillocks to find the *Talking Cricket* and the *Marionette Theater*. From here on the vegetation assumes a different aspect. Leaving behind us clipped hedges of ilex, we enter a *boschetto* of chestnuts and Scotch pines with an underbrush of typically Mediterranean shrubs.

At the crest of the hill is the *Tavern of the fox and the cat*. From here, descending along a path bounded by hedges of cane apple, we note on the left a little olive grove that calls to mind Pinocchio's flight through the fields in search of his two friends.

On the right the vegetation now becomes a dark woods concealing the figures of the *Assassins* who, in Collodi's story, hang Pinocchio to an oak tree. Further on we come upon a clearing in the woods where, in an open, luminous space, the *Child Fairy* stands surrounded by flowers.

At the end of a little valley covered with sweet-smelling roses appears the *House of the Good Fairy* with the bedroom where Pinocchio was created by the three doctors; outside is the *Snail*.

Continuing up another slope that leads to the *Gold coin tree* we find the frightening *Serpent* coming down a path bordered by high walls of laurel and ilex. At the top on the left the *Grown-up Fairy* stands on a little hill; at the bottom of the hill are the *Rabbits carrying a coffin*. Beyond a *boschetto* of bamboo are the *Crab* lying in wait, ready to spray water on visitors, the *Fishnet* and the *Frying Pan* of

the green fisherman, and lastly the *Circus* with Pinocchio transformed into a donkey.

Suddenly, around a sharp curve, appears a magnificent view of the pond with the *Whale*, its enormous

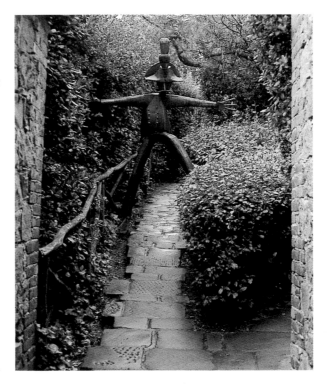

mouth gaping wide open. Inside the whale is *Geppetto*, carrying the *Blue goat* on his back. Lastly Pinocchio, now become a real child, greets visitors inviting them to enter the adventurous world of the pirates, on their ship, in the *Treasure cave* and in the mysterious *Maze*.

The *Carabiniere* by Pietro Consagra

To know more

A. Massa, *I parchi museo di scultura contemporanea*, Florence 1995.

109

Giardino Garzoni

Mazes and waterworks

HOW TO ARRIVE

Not far from Pescia, take the Chiesina Uzzanese exit from highway A11. Privately owned. - Address: Piazza della Vittoria 1, Collodi, Pistoia tel: +39 0572 429590 Visiting hours: every day 9:00 am – 12:00; 2:00 pm – 5:00 pm; 9:00 am – sunset (in summer). Admission: 5,20 €, reduced 3,10 € (6-12 years old and groups of at least 20 persons); Free admission for under 5. Guided visits to be reserved for groups only: 77,00 € in foreign language; 50,00 € in italian. Restrooms - Café Bookshop

The Garzoni garden and villa form a stately, imposing whole. In addition to conserving the last 17th century maze remaining in what was once the State of Lucca, it also boasts a 17th century *parterre de broderie* of exquisitely French taste. Furthermore, its position on a steep hillside (45 meters of difference in altitude) makes this

citrus trees grow along espaliers. Garzoni also created, in the area of the four terraces adjacent to the palazzo, an aviary, a flower garden, and the maze with its grotto. In what is now a *boschetto* of bamboo he placed an orchard with a variety of plants. In the second half of the 18th century a second Romano Garzoni, bearing the same name as the first, transformed the enclosed garden by creating an itinerary in a symbolic/esoteric key. He converted the ancient *romitorio* into the building of the Banetti and added the statue of *Fame*. He enlarged the pond and embell-

The 'garden theater'

estate unique. The hillside rises so steeply before the village of Collodi as to form an indivisible whole with the little town.

In the first half of the 17th century Romano Garzoni laid out a garden consisting of a broad area in the shape of an amphitheater. From here, along the slope, a path leads to terraces immersed in a wood of ilex. The garden is completed by a pond, the little painted chapel of the *romitorio*, a great ilex woods and three terraces where

ished it with decoration; created a lovely water chain with statues and incrustations; changed the 17th century grotto into a cistern providing water for the *giochi d'acqua* of the fountains below, and built the new grotto of Neptune.

Lastly, he constructed the 'garden theater' and the little theater of Pomona. During this same period a *parterre* designed according to French taste was added in the amphitheater area. Garzoni also worked on the Palazzina del

Orologio behind the villa, built according to the indications of Filppo Juvarra.

The entire system of 17th - 18th century gardens has remained unchanged up to the present day, apart from some 19th century replacement of vegetation. After 1842 in fact, Giuseppe Garzoni converted the orchard into a *boschetto* of bamboo, added the palm trees along the avenue of the the encrustations of the water stairway.

The entrance opens onto a broad area in the form of an amphitheater, affording other views of the garden. Tall cypress hedges serve as frame to a group of statues that presage the symbolic messages appearing along the main path through the garden: *Flora, Diana,* the *Fauns, Bacchus* and *Ceres, Apollo* and *Daphne.* This area is dis-

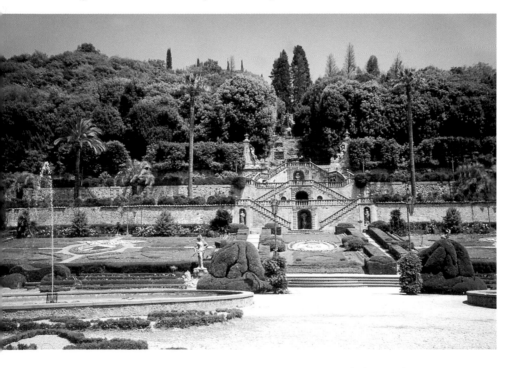

second terrace and made some changes in the avenue of the Emprors.

Itinerary of visit

The first view of the garden appears from the little square in front of the gate, purposely created in the 17th century to provide a broad perspective panorama. Only from here is it possible to observe the perfect harmony between garden and palace, and to discover the anamorphic mascaron half-hidden by tinguished by the *parterre de broderie* as well as by two imposing jets of water in the circular basins. In front, in the sloping *parterre*, appears the Garzoni coat of arms, surrounded by hedges of box and little flower beds framed in lime-mortar.

Above are the thick supporting walls of the three terraces. Adorned with espaliers of citrus trees, they stand out against the complex interwoven ramps of the central stairway. The different levels are

The majestic
stairway

Avenue of Emperors   Statue of *Fame*   Chain of waterfall

Stairway with grottoes

Garzoni Coat of Arms

The garden in an early 20th century photograph

marked by large niches placed on the same axis. The first niche holds the fountain of the *Contadino*, or peasant, pouring water from a barrel. He is flanked by four small niches with the statues of the *Seasons*. The second niche forms an arch leading to the grotto of Neptune, an octagonal area lined in *spugne* with a fountain and water works. In the upper niche is the fountain of the *Villano*, or peasant. He is surrounded by a group of small statues representing monkeys playing ball and two dogs, supplementary elements of the garden's symbolic program.

Above this structure the statues of the two *Satyrs* frame the scene appearing further up: the great 'water chain' with the statue of *Fame* at its top. This part of the garden, called the **Avenue of Emperors**, is perhaps the most striking feature of the park.

At the top of the water stairway is

an avenue of camellias with four oriental sofas and a statue of the *Turk*.

The decoration of the pond, which can be clearly observed from this point, shows obvious cracks created by the designer to represent the effects of an earthquake. It is in fact from the shaking of the earth that the statue of *Fame*, blowing water into the pond below, emerges.

A number of garden paths lead up the hill to the building of the Bagnetti, where the lord and lady and their guests once bathed to music played by a chamber orchestra.

To the left of the avenue of camellias is a gate opening onto a path leading to the palazzo. We then cross the *Ponte sul Rio* with its waterworks controlled from the flower garden above, adorned with the fountains of *Hercules with the Hydra* and *Sampson slaying the Philistine*. From the bridge the works in the **maze** below can be actuated.

We are now in the avenue of the Poor. To the right a gate marks the private area of the garden; to the left a path leads down to the maze with the grotto and to the *boschetto* of bamboo.

From here a narrow wooden bridge returns to the enclosed garden.

After passing the fountain of the Wild Boar we follow the path along the outer edge of the garden to reach the garden theater with its statues of *Comedy* and *Tragedy*.

From here we can take the narrow, half-hidden paths lying between high cypress hedges back to the level part of the garden and the amphitheater.

To know more

F. Gurrieri, *Il giardino e il castello Garzoni a Collodi*, Collodi 1975

J. Chatfield, *A Tour of Italian Gardens*, New York 1988.

V. Cazzato, M. Fagiolo, M.A. Giusti, *Teatri di Verzura. La scena del giardino dal Barocco al Novecento*, II ed., Florence 1995.

Above
The rustic grotto with the statue of the *Contadino*

Top of page
The 'garden theater'

Parco di Celle

An encounter with environmental art

HOW TO ARRIVE

Near Santomato,
along the Via Pistoiese.
Owner:
The Gori Collection.
Address:
Loc. Santomato,
Pistoia
fax: +39 0573 479486
Visiting hours: May –
September only upon
presentation of request
in writing
Restrooms
Bookshop

The Villa of Celle, an imposing Baroque structure, is surrounded by a scenic garden from the same period, consisting of a flower garden and a great orchard of fruit trees. All around, for 25 hectares, extends the 19th century park, arriving as far as the slopes of the distant hills.

The site is magnificent, and nature is bountiful. It may have been this enthralling atmosphere that inspired Giovanni Gambini, commissioned by the owner Caselli around the middle of the 19th century, to lay out an extensive roman-

ronmental art should emerge as the dominating theme.

The contemporary park was created by Giuliano Gori, the present owner, a highly cultured collector. In the early 1980s Celle received the first works of artists who wanted to display their production outdoors, rather than in the restricted space of museums and galleries. Some of the property used as farmland was then subjected to other initiatives, aimed at allowing the surrounding nature to be perceived from a different viewpoint.

A visit to the park is always guided by experts who work with the collection. Significant moments in the history of gardening are discussed, harmoniously interwoven with the viewing of works of contemporary art, extraordinary and versatile. Around many of the works are

Labyrinth
by Richard Morris

tic park and furnish it with an aviary, a tea pavilion, a lake and an *orrido*, or waterfall, according to the Central European fashion of the times. The destiny of the park thus seemed marked. Here, where the power of nature is so magic and so strong, it was only natural that envi-

places of pause that recall the *fabriques* of French 18th century parks: garden furnishings that become architectural spaces and gardens within a garden. *Labyrinth* by Richard Morris (1982), a work in Trani stone and serpentine in two-tone bands, recalls the style of Tus-

Katarsis
by Magdalena
Abakanowicz

Formula Compound
by Dennis
Oppenheim

an Romanic churches. Placed on a gentle slope, it invites the visitor to explore it and experience the sense of bewilderment it inevitably evokes. From a nearby platform the maze can be seen from above, with its triangular plan and inner meanders. **Theme and Variations II** by Fausto Melotti (1981) is one of this great sculptor's most important works. We find it near the little lake in the vicinity of the villa. Eight steel elements six meters high bear chains, spheres and other elements that, moved by the wind, produce sounds of mystic resonance. The

115

Artifice and nature

Just beside the waterfall an epigraph records the work of Giovanni Gambini: "in the years '44 and '45 of the 19th century / this rocky cliff having been built above/the thick wall... / Gio.Gambini of Pistoia, requested to decorate this part of the wood, having completed the island / and the borders of the lake, imagined it, directed it / and without the devices used by art / made it conform to lovely nature / showing itself more original and severe". These words express all the philosophy of the art of romantic gardens: creating "conforming to nature", that is creating works that appear wholly natural even when they are produced by ingenuity, and are therefore artificial.

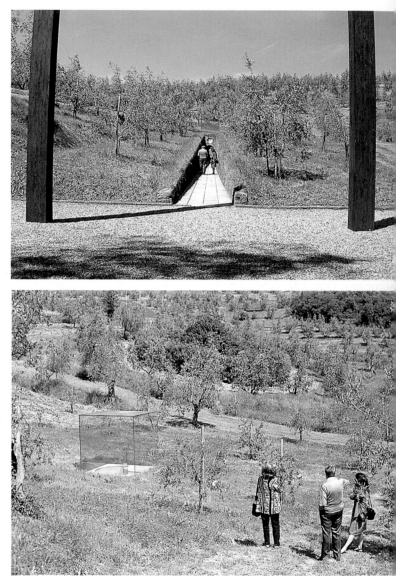

My hole in the sky
by Bukichi Inoue

shape mirrored in the water and the sounds emitted link the work to the surrounding environment in a kind of symbiosis. Between the lake and the tea pavilion the American sculptress Beverly Pepper, exploiting the concave morphology of the terrain, has created a work of art that is midway between sculpture and architecture, *Celle Theater Space*, dedicated to Pietro Porcinai. The stage ends in two backdrops made of cast iron covered with turf, in an installation that is a sort of outdoor theater. The triangular tier of seats ending at the top in two cast iron columns recalling the shape of a diapason, can hold 350 persons. Between 1985 and 1989 the Japanese artist Bukichi Inoue built a symbolic itinerary entitled *My hole in the sky* and installed it along the edge of the park, in the olive grove. From a square piazza a trickling channel of water invites us to traverse a long corridor between two walls of stone. Halfway down the corridor the path is barred by little basin of water. Continuing we enter, according to the artist's intention, the "viscera of the earth", from which we exit by climbing a winding staircase built of white marble. On returning to the surface we find ourselves standing in a glass cube. Jan Hamilton Finlay, an artist and poet who has created many works linked to the garden, chose to position his poetic *Virgilian woods*, created in 1985, outside of the park; little sculptures in bronze appear beside a plow, a basket of fruit and some inscriptions hanging from the branches of the olive trees. Recently the Japanese artist Hidetoshi Nagasawa has constructed a **zen garden** in yellow marble. It is situated beyond a fountain inserted in the corner beside the entrance to the environment/installation.

Celle Theater Space
by Beverly Pepper

At right
Celle Sculpture
by Mauro Staccioli

"If foreseeing the future is a risky game in which man tends by nature to participate, for the collection of the Celle farm we can risk some optimistic predictions based on the deep-rooted presence of its installations, on the programs now being carried out and on the availability of new and ample spaces. The most comforting indications come however from those who, for natural reasons of consanguineous succession, will follow in our footsteps, because they too feel growing within them the same needs and the same curiosity that have urged us in the past to take the most beautiful path from among the many that form the maze of life".

Giuliano Gori, *Introduzione a Arte Ambientale*, Turin 1993.

Villa Bibbiani

A fascinating botanical collection

HOW TO ARRIVE

Between Florence and
Empoli, Montelupo exit
from the Firenze-Pisa-
Livorno highway.
Owner: Giovanna
Donato Del Gratta and
Donatella Marchiafava
Del Gratta
Address: Loc. Bibbiani,
Capraia, Florence
tel.: +39 0571 57338
fax: + 39 0571 979356
e-mail:
bibbiani@penteres.it
www.bibbianifattoria.it
Visiting hours:
by appointment only
(Friday afternoons,
May - September)
Admission: 5,00 €
Partially accessible
to the disabled
Restrooms
Bookshop

An austerely elegant building, its appearance softened only by the graceful formal garden on the southern side, Villa Bibbiani owes its fame to the great park in which it is immersed, one of the most important gardens of acclimatization in Italy (along with those of Villa Hambury at Ventimiglia and Villa Ricasoli on the promontory of the Argentario).

In the park, planned by the famous statement and agronomist Cosimo Ridolfi, numerous botanical species coming from different climates were planted in the early decades

with the park at the desire of his mother Anastasia, who was particularly fond of it. As he wrote in 1843, "I find in the care related to such a pleasant duty a pastime that is both delightful and instructive to which I abandon myself with passionate commitment. My dearest studies seem even sweeter to me amid the impenetrable brush that I am transforming into flowery woods". In short time the garden became famous for its botanical collections. Some of the plants were grown outdoors (particularly interesting are the collections of *Crataegus*, *Eucalyptus*, *Ficus*, and *Magnolia*), some in greenhouses and tepidarium, such as the fine examples of *Cactus* and *Pelargonium*. A role of special importance in Ridolfi's collections was played by camellias (the garden's first catalogue lists a remarkable 195

The formal garden

of the 19th century. Their capacity for adapting to Italian weather and the possibility of using them for both ornamental purposes and forestry could thus be verified. Ridolfi began to occupy himself

species or varieties of camellias) and araucarias. From an araucaria seed sent to Bibbiani by the horticultural establishment Budin of Chambéry was grown a plant recognized by the famous botanist

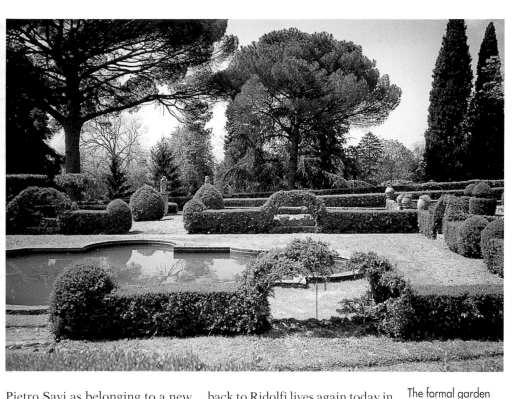

The formal garden

Pietro Savi as belonging to a new species. It was called *Araucaria ridolfiana* in homage to Ridolfi. The park, which may have been designed by Ridolfi himself, covers nearly 20 hectares. Winding paths lead through clumps of brush and sun-lit clearings. The visitor discovers the numerous botanical species still existing today in an alternation of views typical of the 19th century sensitivity for landscape.

The feeling of a romantic park is accentuated by the *fabriques* scattered through the garden, the little buildings that adorn it: the icehouse, the furnace and the arch of Man, an imitation ruin.

The formal garden dates from the early years of the 20th century. It houses a graceful **'garden theater'** divided into parterres of evergreen shrubs and embellished by topiaries and exotic palms.

The collector's tradition harking back to Ridolfi lives again today in the nursery of exotic conifers, where 27 species of rare pines of great ornamental value are grown.

To know more:
G. Moggi, L. Falciani, *Guida botanica al parco di Bibbiani*, Florence 1991.
F. Chiostri, *Parchi della toscana*, Todi 1989.

Chronology

15th c. Bibbiani is the feud of the Frescobaldi family.
1809 Anastasia Frescobaldi asks her son Cosimo, statesman and agronomist, to "render pleasant this estate of Bibbiani, which she loved, how much she could not say, as a paternal keepsake".
1843 Marchese Cosimo Ridolfi publishes the *Catalogo delle piante coltivate a Bibbiani e cenni su qualcuna delle medesime*, listing the numerous species of herbs, shrubs and trees, both exotic and domestic, existing on his property.
1903 The estate is sold to Baron Raimondo Franchetti, who purchases other farms in the direction of Pulignano and gives particular impetus to wine production.
1937 Bibbiani is bought by the Del Gratta family, who are its present owners.

Giardino di Granaiolo

A courageous initiative

HOW TO ARRIVE

Between San Miniato
and Certaldo,
along S.S. 429.
Privately owned.
Address:
Loc. Castelfiorentino,
Florence
tel.: +39 055 570216
(Università inter-
nazionale dell'arte,
Centro studi sul giardi-
no e il paesaggio)
Visiting hours:
by appointment only
and for groups

The tiered lawn

The building as it is today, an imposing parallelepiped surmounted by a central tower, probably results from successive ren-

early anticipation of drastically minimalist themes.

The original project called for the construction of a swimming pool surrounded by a high wall, to the side of the villa. The wall was not built however and the pool appears today as a simple rectangular basin inserted among the trees of the park.

As recalled by Gae Aulenti in a brief text written sixteen years after

ovations carried out by the Pucci family, the long-time owners of the estate. The most recent initiative, dating from 1970, was the work of the architect Gae Aulenti.

The garden appears today of an extreme simplicity. It is formed of a series of **low tiers of turf** bounded by stone curbs. The earthen tiers widen out in front of the villa, modeling the gentle slope before it. This is not only a conceptual revival of the terraced or tiered garden of Tuscan tradition, but also an innovative interpretation that manages to frame the classic construction of the villa in a geometry harmoniously fitted into its context.

Behind the house a **flower border** represents the only concession to color in a project that is based on the essential, and is a remarkably

the Granaiolo project, the new garden took the place of the existing layout in Italian garden style.

"At the turn of the century", recalls the architect, "there had been constructed in front of the house, surrounded by vegetation in the form of *macchia*, an Italian garden with palms, shrubs and fountains that had impaired the harmonious relationship".

The new design for the garden was thus a bold initiative, evidently intended to reconstruct a lost harmony and equilibrium through a decided and to some extent daring gesture that can be seen today as anticipatory. Aulenti adds, "I designed the Tuscan garden of Granaiolo in 1970, and every time I visit it or see it again in a photograph I am amazed that it exists. How it is possible that intelligent

The villa

persons such as my clients believed in the drawings I presented them enough to decide to build that garden?".

This doubt, retrospective, sprung from an awareness of the difficulty of designing a garden destined to change and evolve over the course of time. How was it possible to predict the metamorphosis of a park designed in the severest, strictest geometry into something natural and harmonious? "For myself as well", concludes Aulenti, "although I foresaw the possibility, it was hard to believe in it, so much so that I can today tranquilly declare the risk and definitively decide that I will never design another garden". The original idea of the designer was that of "applying the principle of Land Art, an art that penetrates into the earth,

that impresses on the earth the sign of an expression, and this without repudiating the long tradition of the Italian garden".

Granaiolo thus represents the successful attempt to give shape to an idea, to transcribe the signs of Land Art in the form of a welcoming, comfortable garden, inhabited daily. It is also the entirely concrete proof that one can learn from what exists and skillfully utilize an ancient lesson, integrating it into a language of innovative content.

To know more

G. Aulenti, *Un progetto mediterraneo*, in O. di Collibiano, O. Camerana, I. Origo, G. Aulenti, "Altri giardini, altri orti", Milan 1986.

Villa il Castelluccio

A contemporary masterpiece

HOW TO ARRIVE

Not far from Empoli, the Empoli or Santa Croce sull'Arno exit coming from the Firenze-Pisa-Livorno highway.
Owner: Antonella Costantini Cavini
Address: Via dei Medici 6, Ponte a Cappiano, Fucecchio, Florence
Reservations and information: ancatas@tin.it
Visiting hours: by appointment only (at the owner's discretion) the last week in May, except for holidays, 10:00 – 12:00 am
Accessible to the disabled

The lawn
in front of the house

In the countryside between San Miniato and Fucecchio, around a fine 17th century construction standing on the crest of a little hill, Pietro Porcinai created one of his most mature and complete works in the years between 1971 and 1980.

Thanks to the understanding and collaboration of exceptional clients Porcinai was challenged to express his talent by designing an entire portion of landscape, remodeling the terrain, providing a pond for irrigation, and lastly creating a whole woods.

The design is structured around a long grassy ring road that runs around the hill halfway up, set off by groves of trees, thickets of shrubs and flowering slopes. Within the ring is the garden proper, in close contact with the house.

The entire complex includes a swimming pool covered by an iron-and-glass structure, a tennis court placed in a natural amphitheater, a greenhouse and a parking area with garage.

Itinerary of visit

Along a path through the woods we arrive at the gate to the estate. In traversing an avenue of olive trees we find two box hedges clipped in the shape of pilasters, marking the entrance to the lawn surrounding the house.

The parking area is on the left, embellished by an ingenious play of paving in stone and pebbles alternating with patches of lawn. In front of the villa the lawn is soft-

ly modeled. From here the gaze sweeps over the countryside, and the domesticated landscape drifts off into the natural one around it, framed by a hedge of pomegranates.

Concealed by box shrubs are skylights over the swimming pool below. A splendid **path** leads to the area of the swimming pool, flanked by a silvery escarpment of *teucrium fruticans* and a mixed hedge of laurel and cane apples. Upon entering the garden, beyond the large sliding door that closes it off, we can admire the perfection of the details, the materials and the colors. The tones are the restful ones of wood and terra-cotta, along with the green of ferns, *Ficus*, papyrus and *Ruscus*.

The **pool** is splendid, especially for the contrasting colors of various

materials: black ceramic tesserae on the bottom, white pebbles on the walls. The service areas, for which Porcinai designed the furnishings, link the level of the swimming pool to the house through the basement. Further on, through a glass door, we arrive at the greenhouse; before it, on the lawn stands the bronze sculpture of a sunbathing girl.

Returning to the house we walk through a clump of field maples blazing with color in autumn. On the lowest terrace appears a grove

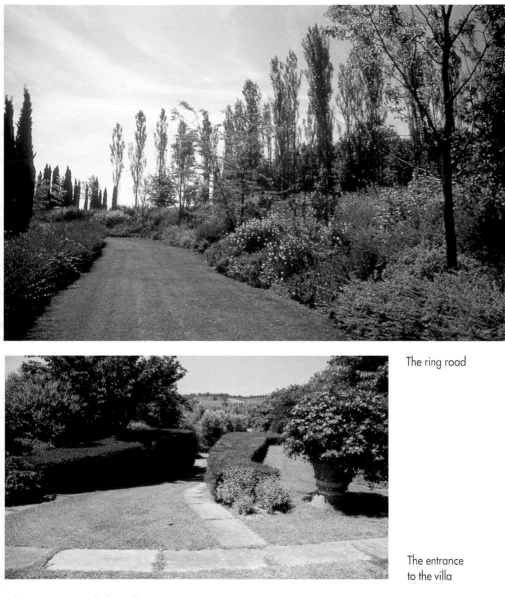

The ring road

The entrance
to the villa

of poplars, a subtle reference to the surrounding landscape. Descending still further we reach the grassy path that runs round the hill; still lower appears an artificial lake around which have been planted reeds, willows, elms and sorbs. In autumn the bright red of the *Taxodium distichum* stands out in vivid contrast to the white tones of the poplars.

To know more
M. Matteini, *Pietro Porcinai architetto del giardino e del paesaggio*, Milan 1991, pp. 202-208.

123

Villa Marlia

An enchanting landscape

HOW TO ARRIVE

Not far from Lucca,
take the Altopascio exit
coming from highway
A11 (Firenze-Mare)
Owner:
the Pecci Blunt family
Address: Marlia, Lucca
tel.: +39 0583 30009
fax: + 39 0583 30108
for reservations also:
villareale@cln.it
Visiting hours:
by appointment only
from December through
February. From March
through November
guided visits every
hour from 10:00 am to
12:00 am and 3:00 pm
to 6:00 pm.
Closed on Mondays
(unless holiday)
Admission: 6,00 €,
reduced 5,00 € (for
groups). Poorly accessible to the disabled
Restrooms

The villa seen from
the lake

At right
Detail of the atrium in
the nymphaeum

The park of the royal villa of Marlia is the most important in the Lucchesia and its complex history of numerous transformations and stratifications makes it extraordinarily interesting (the villa is still today called "royal" coat of arms (1723-1729).

The park, inserted in a magnificent landscape, covers 19 hectares and is divided into three gardens, each dating from a different period - the Baroque garden around the villa and the Palazzina dell'Orologio; the romantic park; and the *art deco* garden laid out in the 1920s.

The Baroque garden, with its imposing *ragnaie*, water theater and *teatro di verzura*, is harmoniously linked to the symphony of colors distinctive of the landscape

because after having been owned by the Grand Duke of Tuscany it became the residence of Vittorio Emanuele II King of Italy).

Within the park are three constructions: Villa Buonvisi Orsetti, around which has been created a remarkable Baroque garden; the 18th century Palazzina dell'Orologio, on the same axis as the great *ragnaia* of the first garden; and Villa del Vescovo, now uninhabited, built in the 16th century over an existing structure owned by the Archbishop of Lucca. The latter villa, surrounded by an important garden with nymphaeum, bears on the door the Bernardino Guinigi

124

portion, abounding in rare and exotic plants. Contributing to the striking effect of the whole is the garden of Jacques Gréber, created in the early 20th century according to the model of the Islamic water garden.

The 'garden theater'

The modern garden by Jacques Gréber

Itinerary of visit

The Baroque garden surrounds the villa in a harmoniously linked pattern of separate sectors. From the exedra at the entrance we arrive at the long rectangular lawn from which the villa appears in all its elegance. Continuing to the left we enter the avenue that leads through the ancient *ragnaia*, formed of high

125

hedges of laurel and ilex; at the end of the avenue appears the lovely facade of the Palazzina dell'Orologio.

From the avenue through the *ragnaia*, to the right, a beautiful gate leads to the lemon garden. It is divided into four sectors, each of them framing a great magnolia tree.

To the south the garden is closed off by a niche with fountain. To the north a semicircular ramp of stairs leads to the ornamental fishpond

Lake

At right:
The Palazzina dell'Orologio

The lemon garden

Detail of the water theater

with statues of the rivers *Arno* and *Serchio*; at the end is a lovely nymphaeum with a statue of *Leda and the Swan*. In homage to Leda, a pair of swans lives in the rectangular pool.

Through a circular garden room with waterworks and fountain, a path transverse to the fishpond leads to the *teatro di verzura*. Built of yew and box, it is designed like a real theater. At the back of the stage, three terra-cotta statues of *Colombina*, *Pantalone* and *Balanzone* pay homage to the tradition of the *Commedia dell'Arte*.

From the fishpond we return toward the villa. Behind the building a broad semicircular basin marks the boundary of the garden while linking the park and villa to the hills in the background.

The **water theater**, a vivid Baroque scenario of water, stone and vegetation, is a recurrent element in the villas of the Lucchesia. The nearby Villa Grabau as well as Villa Oliva have similar features, designed to confer greater solemnity on the space.

The water theater

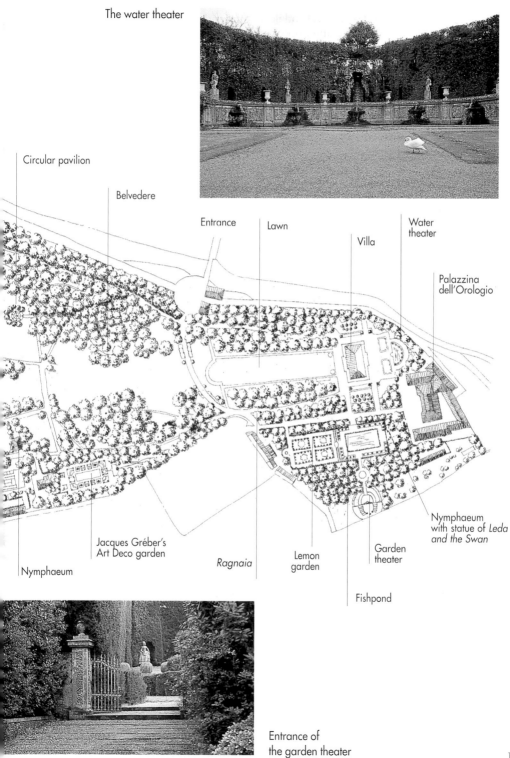

Circular pavilion

Belvedere

Entrance

Lawn

Villa

Water theater

Palazzina dell'Orologio

Nymphaeum with statue of *Leda and the Swan*

Jacques Gréber's Art Deco garden

Ragnaia

Lemon garden

Garden theater

Nymphaeum

Fishpond

Entrance of the garden theater

Enlarging the property by purchasing the nearby Villa del Vescovo, Elisa Baciocchi managed to create one of the finest 19th century parks in all Tuscany. Favored by the beauty of the site, the rich soil and

where there is the best view of the villa. In autumn the blazing colors of the great red oaks, the beech trees, the tulip trees and gingko offer an unforgettable spectacle On the left, climbing the slope, we

The fishpond;
in the background,
the fountain with the
statue of *Leda and
the Swan*

Next page
Detail of the topiaries
near the villa

the climate itself, the unknown designer of the park (undoubtedly influenced by the ideas expressed by Jean Marie Morel in the treatise *Théorie des jardins*, published at Paris in 1776), skillfully harmonized the existing formal gardens with the new romantic park. The alternation of irregular lawns, of open and closed areas, creates a varied scenario that concludes with the lower lake, from

find a modern circular pavilion entirely surrounded by a pergol of wisteria.
Continuing beyond the hillock/be vedere, created to afford a view c the park from above, we ca admire the extraordinary flower ing of the **camellia woods**.
On the right is the Villa del Vesco vo, erected on a monumental bas with niches and statues. The for mal garden was renovated at th

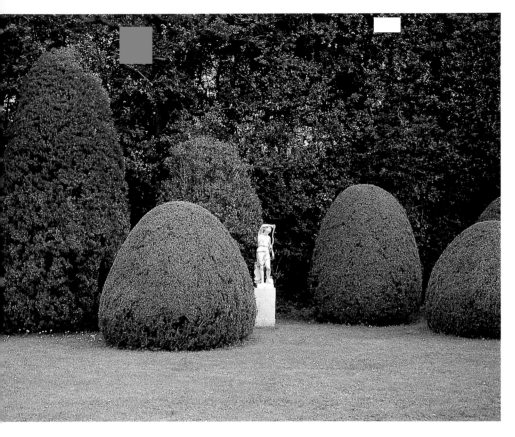

turn of the century. The 16th century **nymphaeum** appears as a splendid pavilion preceded by a loggia. Entirely decorated in grotesque designs, the nymphaeum is composed of an atrium with terra-cotta and pebble flooring and an octagonal room with vaulted ceiling, where three niches hold fountains adorned by sea gods.

Returning from the nymphaeum to the villa, on the right we reach an area of the park transformed in the 1920s.

Here the French landscape artist Jacques Gréber created a games area with an unusual swimming pool and a **formal garden** inspired by Islamic water gardens, according to the *art deco* style then in vogue. The garden, rectangular in shape, seems carved out of the sur-rounding vegetation and is distinguished by brightly colored plants and flowers. Hedges of *euonimo*, with their yellow-green leaves, contrast with brightly flowering hibiscus and bougainvillea.

The bougainvillea plants are dug up and moved to the greenhouse each year, to be planted outdoors again in springtime. This practice, complicated and expensive, clearly shows the demanding and refined nature of Gréber's project.

To know more

Architetture del verde. Le Ville gentilizie lucchesi e il loro territorio, edited by M. Vannucchi, Lucca 2000.

Chronology

16th c. The villa is built by the Buonvisi family.

1651 After the bankruptcy of the Buonvisi, the villa passes to the Orsetti family. The garden is renovated in Baroque style.

1805 Elisa Baciocchi, Napoleon's sister, becomes the sovereign of Lucca. She creates the romantic park with the acquisition of the Villa del Vescovo and its gardens. The twin pavilions are created on the piazzale with exedra at the entrance.

1918 Sold by the Borbone family, the villa becomes the property of the Pecci Blunt family.

129

Villa Mansi

Baroque waterworks

HOW TO ARRIVE

In the vicinity of Capannori, near the Capannori exit from highway A11 (Firenze-Mare)
Owner:
Claudia Salom
Address:
Via delle Selvette, 242, Segromigno in Monte Capannori, Lucca
tel.: +39 0583 920234
fax: + 39 0583 928114
www.villamansi.it
Visiting hours: every day except Monday,
10:00 am – 6:00 pm
Admission: 6,50 €, reduced 5,50 €
(for groups of at least 20)

The park of Villa Mansi was built in successive eras. The harmony with which the various initiatives have been carried out over the course of time has resulted in an ensemble of unique beauty, containing a vast range of plant species.

In the 16th century the garden was first laid out with terraces and geometric beds extending around the villa. The Renaissance park was then transformed in the 18th century, probably by Filippo Juvarra. The only feature of the 18th century initiative that remains today is the 'water chain', which runs through the length of park, flanked by hedges and statues of human or animal figures.

The chain of little waterfalls ends in the broad octagonal basin that was the fulcrum of Juvarra's design. The formal *boschetto* was in fact planted in the shape of a star radiating out from with the little square containing the basin.

From here the water flowed on to a **fishpond** of elegant design decorated with balustrades and statues. Georg Cristoph Martini (1685-1745), a guest at Villa Mansi, described the area around the fishpond in his *Viaggio in Toscana*: "Near the palace, on the right hand is the so-called fishpond where fish are kept, into which statues personifying the rivers pour water. Around the pool run magnificent paths lined with hedges and a majestic walk between great elms and other trees.

I slept in a chamber that opened just onto this *boschetto*, and listened all night to the exquisite

The *boschetto* of banana trees behind the villa

music of the nightingales that nest there in great number".

Beside the basin, in the direction of the villa, once stood the secret garden, a space isolated by a wall where flowers blossomed in geometric *parterres*.

The visual fulcrum of the garden was the 'Bath of Diana', a pond with an imitation ruin with statues of the goddess of hunting and a swimming water-nymph. As a result of the 19th century transformation of a portion of the garden into an English park, the Bath of Diana is now isolated within a *boschetto*.

Other additions made during the Romantic period include the broad lawn in front of the villa that heightens the effect of the imposing residence. The splendid facade should be observed from a distance, at the top of the gently sloping lawn, surrounded by romantic woods and brightened in autumn by the colors of the *Liriodendrun tulipifera*.

Surrounding the lawn is the **romantic woods**, where some exotic species grow (*Cedrus atlantica, Picea abies, Pseudotsuga menziesii* and *Chamaecyparis lawsoniana*).

On the eastern side of the villa is a path lined with palm trees and a *boschetto* of bamboo. To the west of the building is a fine collection of camellias containing many rare varieties.

The fishpond

The 'water chain'

To know more

A. Brilli, *Viaggiatori stranieri in terra di Lucca*, Milan 1996 (the quotation form Georg Cristoph Martini is on p. 97).

131

Villa Torrigiani

The garden of Flora

A majestic avenue of ancient cypresses leads to the magnificent villa standing in a fine position at the foot of the hills. In this part of the Lucchesia a splendid succession of villas and gardens forms a landscape unique the world over for elegance and beauty.

The original plan of the garden dates back to the 16th century, when the Buonvisi family owned the estate. In the first half of the 17th century the new owner Nicolao Santini, ambassador from Luc-

attributed to the hand of Le Nôtre although certain documentation is lacking. The elegant design of the *parterres* and the broad stretches of water in front of the villa and behind it reveal the strong influence of French taste.

The Arcadian poet Filandro Cretense (pseudonym of Antonio Cerati), after visiting the villa described the garden in his *Ville lucchesi*, published in 1783: "a most pleasant lawn, crowned with green espaliers, opens at the end of a broad road lined with cypresses, providing a fine horizon to the facade of the palace. On the opposite side appears an atrium beyond which stretches an exquisite garden; and two fountains at the same distance share the honor of embell-

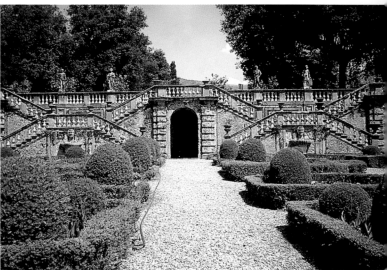

The garden of Flora

ca to the court of Louis XIV, transformed the garden, inspired by the splendor of French style.

In 1816 the villa becomes property of the Torrigiani family, after the marriage between Vittoria Santini and the marchese Pietro Guadagni Torrigiani.

Some 18th century *cabrei*, or maps, illustrate the Baroque layout, often

ishing the uniformity of those flourishing plains".

Remaining from the 17th century garden are the two great pools or the lawn before the villa, the **garden of Flora** and the nympheaum or Grotto of the Winds, to the right of the main building. The Baroque garden is structured along an axis that includes the fishpond above

The villa

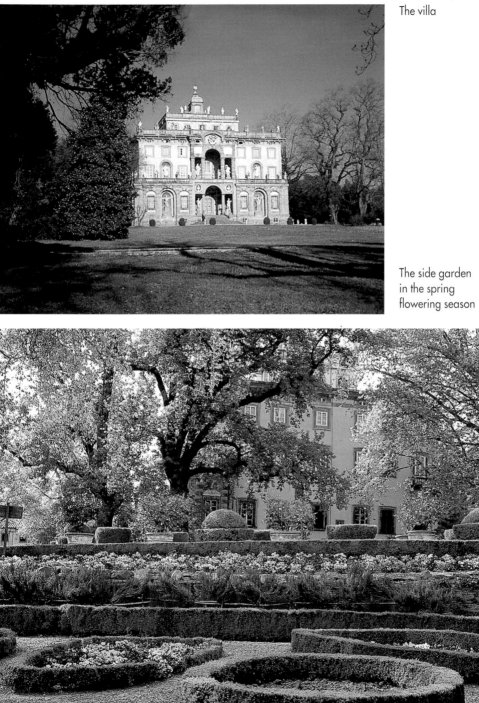

The side garden
in the spring
flowering season

and the garden of Flora, a rare example of Baroque flower garden, on the lower level. The two levels are connected by a system of stairways adorned with statues and vases. The Garden of Flora can be entered by passing behind the villa and then descending, or by entering directly from the garden

17th century basins

Camellias

The avenue of cypresses

level and then climbing a stairway leading to the top of the fishpond. A lovely area adorned with flowers is bounded by walls and enhanced by the geometry of the beds planted with hedges and spheres of clipped box. To the south the garden ends at the

Entrance

The upper pool

Villa | Fishpond | Side garden | 19th century woods | Garden of Flora | Nymphaeum

The garden of Flora

nymphaeum, an octagonal pavilion with a dome crowned by the statue of *Flora*, decorated with wrought-iron masks and flowers. In the nymphaeum the waterworks were once so spectacular as to induce Filandro Cretense to praise hydraulics, the science that allowed such marvels to exist. In the niches stand seven statues of the *Winds*. The splendid pavement of black and white pebbles, with its spiral pattern, is striking. A portion of the Baroque garden was replaced by the 19th century park. The variety of the trees is remarkable, in particular for the majestic *Liriodendron tulipifera*, the tulip tree, and the so-called bald cypress (*Taxodium distichum*). The collection of camellias is also important for its 19th century varieties.

To know more

I. Belli Barsali, *Ville e committenti dello stato di Lucca*, Lucca 1979.

M. Fagiolo, M.A. Giusti, *La stella e la rosa. Analisi della Villa Buonvisi Santini a Camigliano*, in "Il giardino delle Muse. Arti e artifici nel Barocco europeo", edited by M.A. Giusti and A. Tagliolini, Florence 1995.

Villa Buonvisi Oliva
Water music

HOW TO ARRIVE

In the vicinity of Marlia, Lucca or Capannori exit coming from highway A11 (Firenze-Mare)
Owner: Luisa Oliva
Address:
San Pancrazio, Lucca
tel.: +39 0583 406462
fax: +39 0583 406771
Visiting hours:
9:30 am – 12:30 pm, 2:30 pm – 6 pm from March 15 to Nov. 15.
Visits are possible by appointment also in the closing time.
Admission: 5,00 € for groups of at least 20 persons; 4,00 € over 20 persons

The garden that surrounds Villa Oliva at San Pancrazio, celebrated in the 18th century by Filandro Cretense (pseudonym of the Arcadian poet Antonio Cerati), elegantly reiterates many elements typical of the gardens surrounding the Lucchese villas.

The mansion, standing in a dominant position north of the weir, is the fulcrum of a composition organized around the main axis of the long entrance avenue. To the left of the entrance extends the agricultural area, destined to the cultivation of fruit trees and vineyards. It is laid out in a system of terraces rising toward the villa, which was originally the center of an economic organization based on agriculture. At Villa Oliva, the garden structure is particularly

interesting; the system of terraces is not parallel, but rather perpendicular, to the facade of the villa. This gave rise to the need for a transverse connection realized through the 'water chain' of the *Cascatelle*.

To the right of the avenue, supported by a grassy escarpment, is the formal section of the park, originally divided into regular beds (no longer distinguishable today due to the 19th century transforma-

"It [the garden] is situated on a broad rise so that there extends before it a most lovely perspective of lakes, rivers, woods, hills and populated villages, which things Nature with seductive disorder reunites, forming so to say an immense gallery of animated pictures".

Filandro Cretense, *Le Ville Lucchesi*, 1783.

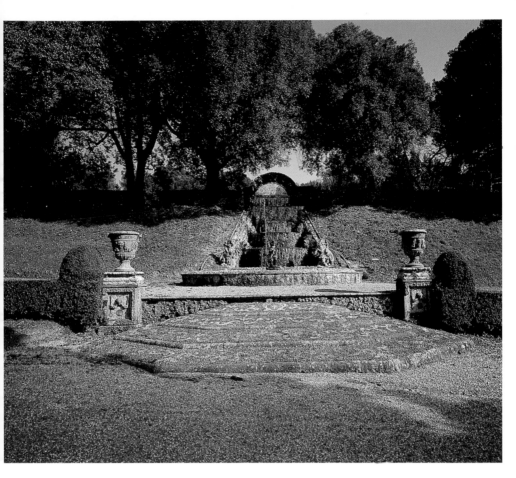

tions). This section contained the *boschetto*, the *ragnaia* and the garden proper. The compact volume of the villa, of austere late 16th century style, opens at the back, toward the hillside, through a magnificent portico facing on a broad semicircular space. This exedra, an element often found at the end of the weir in many Lucchese villas, is planted to lawn and bordered by potted citrus trees. The curved background, formed of a compact hedge of ilexes, opens at the center to show a rustic grotto decorated with calcareous concretions, stalactites and tufa.

The Baroque plan of the garden has remained unaltered and the 19th century changes are superimposed on the original structure, which can still be distinguished. Today the villa is embellished by a collection of tall trees, in the 19th century Lucchese style: monumental cedars, magnolias, gingkos and horse chestnuts.

Itinerary of visit

A visit to the garden starts from the side entrance with its two monumental decorated pillars (in front of the parking lot). We find ourselves behind the villa that opens onto the grandiose **loggia** by Matteo Civitali. Framing the great elliptical lawn with the fountain of the Angel is a backdrop of ilexes that blends harmoniously with the hills behind it, with a rustic grotto at its

The waterfalls
before the pool
of the Amorini

Preceding page
The statue of the
Pitocco

The fountain
of the Siren

The garden in front
of the villa

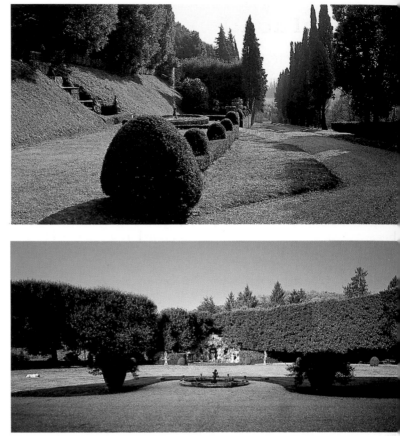

The backdrop
of ilexes

center. We continue toward the beautiful stables, now used for ceremonies, up to the modern swimming pool. On the parapet is a terra-cotta statue of the *Pitocco*.

Upon arriving at the villa we find opening out before us an extraordinary network of gardens laid out on three different levels - the upper level with its *boschetto* of ilexes and pool surrounded by flower beds, a section that was transformed in the 19th century; the central level with a long avenue of ilex and cypress leading to the main entrance, the pool of the Amorini, the fountain of the Cascatelle and the *Kaffeehaus*; last comes the lower level, with the **gallery of hornbeams** and the farm area. The fountain of the Cascatelle is the first of three fountains placed along the 'water chain'.

The other fountains, placed in the wall encircling the weir, are the fountain of Abundance, not far from the *limonaia*, and the splendid **Fountain of the Siren**, surmounted by the coat of arms of the Buonvisi family.

To know more

I. Belli Barsali, *La villa a Lucca dal XV al XIX secolo*, Rome 1964.
I. Belli Barsali, *Ville e committenti dello stato di Lucca*, Lucca 1979.
Giardini e parchi lucchesi nella storia del paesaggio italiano, edited by A. Maniglio Calcagno, Lucca 1992.

Villa Grabau

Trees play the leading role

Villa Grabau appears at the end of a long avenue leading from the fine gate marking the entrance to the property. The garden, covering an area of nine hectares situated on a plain at the foot of the Pizzorne hills, was created in successive stages and is surrounded by farmland.

The villa has been owned by the Grabau family since 1868. Built in late Renaissance style presumably near the end of the 16th century (as replacement for a previous Gothic building), it was renovated in neo-classic style in the 19th centu-

ry. Arriving at the villa by a ring path running around the lawn, we pass through halls frescoed with fine *trompe l'oeil* designs to arrive at the back, where the main perspective axis is further developed and refined. Here we find the **formal garden**, laid out in two levels separated by a stone balustrade decorated with mosaics and fountains. On the upper level, along the borders of two great lawns, stands the collection of lemon trees. At the back a circular fountain and a backdrop of evergreens conceal the entrances to the *selvatico*. The

HOW TO ARRIVE

In the vicinity of Marlia, Lucca or Capannori exit coming
from highway A11 (Firenze-Mare)
Owners: Francesca and Federico Grabau.
Address:
Via di Matraia 269, San Pancrazio, Lucca
tel. and fax: +39 0583 406098 - For information and reservations:
villagrabau@mclink.it
www.villagrabau.it
Visiting hours:
from Nov. 2 to Easter only on Sunday, 11:00 am - 1:00 pm and 2:30 pm - 5:30 pm.
Visits are possible only for groups and by appointment during the closing time.
Admission:
4,20 € for the park, 5,50 € for the park and villa.
Reductions for groups.
Free admission under 12.
Luncheons and tasting of typical products by reservation.
Accessible to the disabled
Restrooms
Bookshop

Great trees in the park

The villa seen
from the entrance

The garden
furnishings

splendid Baroque wall/fountain separating the two levels is built of local Matraia stone and white marble and is decorated with rock crystal, foundry materials, quartz and tufa. Four bronze masks emerge from the wall, spouting water into four semicircular pools. The design, elegant and expressive, has led art historians to attribute the satyrs' heads to Pietro Tacca, one of the finest interpreters of Flo-

rentine Mannerism. The second level of the garden is reached by climbing the little stairway in the center of the wall, guarded by a pair of marble dogs.

In front of the villa extends the English park created in the 19th century, probably in two successive stages. Known for its important botanical collection, the romantic garden has a *boschetto* of bamboo, a *Montagnola* or hillock, and a great circular lawn that enhances the view of the villa. The collection of exotic conifers and broad-leaf trees offers a scenario of remarkable beauty, especially in autumn.

Two great red beech trees, to the right of the villa, cover the lawn with a carpet of bright leaves. On the left conifers and a great tulip tree form a variegated backdrop. Within the woods, in the northern part, a strange grotesque figure carved in stone stands in a clearing. Formerly placed at the center of the circular fountain in the formal garden, it represents a tortoise, the animal sacred to the god Pan, bearing a dragon with a human head and a mask at the back.

On the eastern side of the formal garden is the winter greenhouse; on the western side, the *limonaia*. Recently restored, the *limonaia* provides shelter in winter for the over 100 lemon trees in the park. It has a splendid facade, with seven rustic work portals and seven oval windows standing out against the Pompeian red of the plaster. Inside the building is a wall fountain with the head of Bacchus and a table listing the precise locations of all of the citrus plants to be sheltered during cold weather. On the western side of the villa is a 'garden theater' in boxwood.

Above
The *limonaia*, interior

Top of page
The *limonaia*, exterior

To know more
I. Belli Barsali, *La villa a Lucca dal XV al XIX secolo*, Rome 1964.
Giardini e parchi lucchesi nella storia del paesaggio italiano, edited by A. Maniglio Calcagno, Lucca 1992.

Villa Massei

A Garden in Lucca

HOW TO ARRIVE

Not far from Lucca,
taking the Capannori
exit from highway A11
(Firenze-Mare)
Owners: Gil Cohen
and Paul Gervais
Address:
Via della Chiesa 53,
Massa Macinaia,
Lucca
fax: +39 0583 90138
www.agardeninlucca.com
Visiting hours:
By appointment only
and for groups.
Guided visits.
Admission: 10,00 €
Not accessible to the
disabled

Although dreams only rarely come true, the one of Paul Gervais and Gil Cohen has done so: to live in a villa with a magnificent garden at the gates of Lucca. In a book dedicated to Villa Massei Paul Gervais recalls his splendid adventure. The villa is a 16th century hunting lodge that once belonged to Count Sinibaldi. Almost austere in design, the building is embellished by the loggia behind it, newly opened and restored. The modern garden was created by its two owners from Boston starting in 1982. Over the existing structure of the formal garden, containing a nymphaeum and a series of terraces descending along the sides of the entrance road, they have created a succession of garden rooms. The lawns at the sides of the road are sprinkled with lovely wild flowers. In the lawns, divided by channels filled with water, are collection pools revealing the interesting hydraulic system that was undoubtedly responsible for the agricultural prosperity of the area. The entrance avenue leads to the villa. In front of the elegant brick-red facade an ancient camellia tree, on the right, bears witness to the importance of the plantations that once stood in the garden. The effect of the building is heightened by a broad flower-bordered lawn where greens and whites alternate in exquisite harmony.

The owners experiment with new plants and different methods of growing them. On the northern side of the villa, around the doorway, is a green arch created with the delicate foliage of the *Muelenbeckia complexa*. On either side of the doorway are vases covered with the drooping foliage of *Buxus hallendii*. A late Victorian rose that flowers abundantly, 'La Follette' climbs over the nearby trees.

New gardens planned with sensitivity and intelligence fill the existing spaces, presenting a vegetation so rich as to form a true botanical collection.

The rose garden, an area of transition leading to the garden rooms, is splendid for its fine collection of antique roses (such as the perfumed 'Cuisse de Nymphe Emue', the red 'Cardinal de Richelieu' and the pink 'Souvenir de la Malmaison') alternating with modern roses produced by the famous English nursery of David Austin. Outstanding among the garden rooms are the one dedicated to the Italian garden, laid out six years ago by Paul Gervais with sixteen beds of box and plantings of 'Heavenly Blue' *Caryopteris x clandonensis*. Going on to the orchard, an avenue of thirty-six 'Rennes du Marché' cherry trees suggests a country walk that is beautiful in any season. A natural park bright with spontaneous flowers concludes the series of gardens. Further on a new garden (called 'the serpentine') has been started with some plants

The villa
and the great
camellia

growing along a winding path. Near the swimming pool is the Mediterranean garden, where every two years the *Geranium naderense* comes into bloom. Before a little building is a formal garden surrounded by rosemary hedges. Botanical curiosities of modern taste alternate with memories from the past; for example, the great camphor tree with its perfumed leaves bears witness to the 19th century fashion for exotic plants, widespread in the Lucchesia area.

The magnificent tree dominates the space behind the villa, where the nymphaeum is framed by a pergola of wisteria. The composition is completed by hydrangeas of various species and a border of peonies.

To know more
P. Gervais, *A Garden in Lucca*, New York 2000.

Above
The garden in front of the villa

Top of page
The Italian garden

143

Palazzo Pfanner

The garden of the four elements

HOW TO ARRIVE

At the center of Lucca.
Owners:
The Pfanner family
Address:
Via degli Asili 33,
Lucca
tel.: (tourist information
city hall of Lucca)
+39 0583 583150
fax: +39 0583 991667
Visiting hours: every
day from March to
November,
10:00 am – 6:00 pm
(with seasonal varia-
tions)
Admission:
for villa and park
4,00 €,
reduced 1,00 €
(children 6 to 12,
over 65, groups of at
least 10 persons),
2,50 € for park only.
Accessible to the
disabled
Restrooms

Near Piazza San Frediano in Lucca, set like a jewel between the bastions of the walls and the 18th century palazzo, is a splendid Baroque garden abounding in statues and fascinating views. The beauty of the whole was undoubtedly one of the reasons why the director Jane Campion decided to shoot some of the outdoor scenes for her film *Portrait of a Lady*, taken from the book by Henry James, on the premises of this villa.

The central section of the garden is arranged along the perspective axis indicated by statues of divinities and mythological heroes. On either side of the entrance, in two niches, stand the statues of *Cybele*

of Water. In the background, along the city wall, runs the long *limonaia* now abandoned, its elegant brick facade rhythmically broken by great windows alternating with laurel hedges. At the center of the facade two lions flank a basilisk the emblem of the Controni family. Although the garden at first sight appears as a *hortus conclusus*, in reality the interior space is always in contact with the tree-lined wall of the city and with the urban fabric as a whole.

In the second half of the 17th century the Moriconi family undertook the construction of the palace and began to lay out the garden. Toward the end of the 17th century the Controni family, who had become the owners of the property, embellished it with the construction of the splendid exterior stairway.

With its system of arches and balustrades, the stairway provided a new scenic backdrop.

The garden looking toward the palazzo

and *Hercules*. At the center is an **octagonal pool** with the statues of the *Four Elements*: Vucan represents Fire, Mercury is the symbol of Air, Dionysus of Earth, Oceanus

In 1860 the property was bought by Felice Pfanner, an industrialist of German origin who built a beer factory there, which was to remain open until 1929. The garden was ncluded in the production facilities, and was used for beer tasting (both palace and garden still belong to the Pfanner family).

Itinerary of visit

The garden can be approached from two different directions; either by walking along the path on top of the city walls and suddenly discovering it beyond the Abside of San Frediano, or by passing through the doorway in Via degli Asili opening in a severe facade that gives no hint of the marvels concealed behind it. The half-shadow of a deep portico opens out into the garden with its statues.

At the center of the path is an octagonal pool in masonry, partially modified by the rock garden beds placed next to the main body. The pool, surrounded by a wide border of box, is equipped with an interesting hydraulic system (the circular underground basins can still be seen). The other section of the garden is formed of broad lawns thickly scattered with potted lemons; some still bear the date 1843. Along the sides of the formal garden are tall hedges of laurel and box and two *boschetti* of bamboo originating in the 19th century.

To know more

Lucca segreta. Giardini e orti della città murata, edited by M. Vannucchi, Lucca 1997, pp. 142-143.

The fountain at the center of the garden

145

Giardino dei Tarocchi

A game or a philosophy of life?

HOW TO ARRIVE

Between Capalbio
and Garavicchio,
Chiarone exit in the
direction of Pescia
Fiorentina when
coming from
S.S. 1 Aurelia.
Owner:
Fondazione Il Giardino
dei Tarocchi
Address: Garavicchio,
Capalbio, Grosseto
tel.: +39 0564 895122
fax: +39 0564 895700
Visiting hours: from
mid-May to the
end of October,
2:30 pm - 7:00 pm
By appointment only
and upon presentation
of request in writing for
groups of at least 15
persons at other
seasons.
Admission: 10,50 €,
reduced 6,00 €
(under 12, over 65).
Free admission for the
disabled and under 7
Accessible to the dis-
abled
Restrooms
Bookshop

Niki de Saint Phalle had been trying for years to make a dream come true: to create a garden that would hold all of the personage and places of the tarot cards, become the symbol of her artistic and existential life.

Within the space of an old stone quarry owned by the Caracciolo family, against the background of the Maremma landscape where Tuscany borders on Lazio, her dream became reality in the years between 1979 and 1996. The park came to life through the laborious construction of the 22 figures of the greater Mysteries, which are both sculpture and architecture, monuments and houses to live in. Amid the Mediterranean *macchia* these 'creatures' slowly came to life, some of remarkable size, made of reinforced concrete, covered in mirrors and different types of mosaic and ceramics. With ardent enthusiasm the artist directs a team as numerous as it is heterogeneous of craftsmen, artists, decorators, ceramists and artist friends.

Isolation from the outside world is ensured by the barrier at the entrance, intended to provide a severe and linear break. Created by Mario Botta in 1996, it is made of blocks of tufa. To enter the fantastic world of the tarot cards visitors must confront this barrier, passing through the great circular opening.

Many of the figures can be penetrated, walked over or even lived in, as in the case of the great sphinx that represents the *Empress*. Within its capacious belly, lined by thousands of fragments of mirror, Niki de Saint Phalle lived for months while the garden was being created. In the presence of the sphinx a riddle-question may arise, "If life is a game of cards we are born without knowing the rules. In spite of this we are all called upon to play a hand. Are the tarot figures only a game or do they point the way to a philosophy of life?"

Itinerary of visit

For visiting the garden, no particular itinerary is better than any other. We may let ourselves be guided by Niki De Saint Phalle herself who, in her *Garden of the Tarocchi*, leads us from the figure of the *Magician* to that of the *Papess* and then on to the fountain of the *Wheel of Fortune*, created by the French artist Jean Tinguely.

Along the border of the pool we come upon *Force*, represented by a delicate girl dominating a dragon. Passing under the arch of the bird of *Sun* we find in sequence *Death*, *Devil* and the *World*. After having seen the *Madman* and the *Pope* we walk around the *Hanged Man*, in his colorful house filled with mirrors. On the white ceramic tiling can be seen drawings and sketches for the *Wheel of Fortune* and the *Sun*. In the center of a clearing is *Justice*, with his prisoner.

At the edge of the woods the figures of the *Sweethearts* symbolize *Choice*, while from the *macchia* emerge two solitary figures: the *Hermit* and his enigmatic feminine counterpart, the *Oracle*. From the treetops emerges another figure gleaming with mirrors. It is the *Tower of Babel* struck by lightening, symbolized by the sculpture of Jean Tinguely. Just beside the tower is the *Emperor*, the card of male power. It is a complex and

The *Wheel of Fortune* by Jean Tinguely and, in the background, other sculpture/installations.

ascinating structure, to be visited at leisure. The *Empress* dominates the garden; the enormous sphinx holds within it the *Wagon*, the *Star* and the *Judgement*. Outside is the enchanted area of the chapel of *Temperance* and further on, among the bushes of the Mediterranean *macchia*, the *Moon*.

To know more

VV. AA., *Niki de Saint Phalle. Il giardino dei Tarocchi*, catalogue of the exhibition. Orbetello, Polveriera Guzman, 1997, Milan 1997.

Niki de Saint Phalle, *Il giardino dei Tarocchi*, Berna 1997.

E-mail: tarotg@tin.it

Web: www.nikidesaintphalle.com

"The garden of the Tarocchi is not just my garden, it belongs to all those who have helped me to complete it. I am the architect of this garden. I have imposed my vision because I could not do otherwise. This garden has been created with difficulty, with wild enthusiasm, with obsession and more than anything else, with faith. Nothing and no one could have stopped me. As in all fables, along the path that leads to the hidden treasure I have encountered dragons, witches, magicians and the Angel of Temperance".

Niki de Sant Phalle

The garden of Daniel Spoerri

The play of affinities

HOW TO ARRIVE

Take S.S. 2 Cassia headed toward Rome and turn off after Castiglion d'Orcia.
Owner: Fondazione Il Giardino
Address: Loc. Giardino, Seggiano, Grosseto
tel.: +39 0564 950457
fax: +39 0564 950026
www.ilgiardinodi-danielspoerri.it
patriziacianchi@libero.it
Visiting hours: from July 1 to Sept. 15,
4:00 pm to 8:00 pm, from Sept. 16 to Oct. 31, 3:00 pm to 7:00 pm from Easter to Sept. 1 open in the weekends.
By appointment only in other seasons.
Admission: 7,00 €, reduced 5,00 €
Guided visits by reservation 104,00 €
Restrooms - Café
Bookshop

Paradiso, that is, garden, was the name of the place up to two hundred years ago, and the beauty of this garden stretched out over the splendid hillside facing the town of Seggiano is truly heavenly. A fine avenue of ancient plane trees leads to the villa and already in the parking lot the visitor is surrounded by the works of Daniel Spoerri and other artists. The most significant characteristic of this garden of art is to be found in the elective affinities that have linked the Swiss artist to other artists spiritually akin to him. The itinerary, marked by works of

Spoerri the chance for an intense confrontation with the nature of the place. From this came the idea of displaying works of art outdoors, distributing them along an itinerary similar to that of the sacred woods of Bomarzo, near Viterbo. The garden, which became a Foundation in 1997, has been the site of exhibitions since 1998, when the first show was held, entitled *The Friends of Daniel Spoerri's Garden*. From the entrance we proceed toward the great meadow where some of Spoerri's works can be seen: *The Warriors of the Night*, the *Labyrinthine Walled Path*, and the *Grass Divan*. From here the path leads on to the most panoramic point, overlooking the town of Seggiano, where we find another work by Spoerri, *Unicorns/The Navel of the World*. Continuing along the ring walk, we find one of the most sig-

*The Warriors
of the Night*
by Daniel Spoerri

art, winds around the villa and through the broad meadow in front of the woods without any precise theme, but following creations brought together by a common intention. The garden contains 63 works by artists including, in addition to Spoerri himself, Eva Aeppli, Roberto Barni, and Roland Topor. The purchase of a large estate gave

nificant works in the collection *Chambre No 13 de l'Hotel Carcassonne Paris 1959-1965*, a representation in bronze of the room in which Spoerri worked during the years indicated in the title.

To know more:
Il Giardino di Daniel Spoerri, edited by A. Mazzanti, 1998-99

Parco della Sterpaia

An art itinerary through the woods

The itinerary of the monumental forest of Sterpaia represents one of the most recent initiatives in Tuscany to combine elements of naturalist interest with an art itinerary.

This woods, a rare survival of what was once the typical coastal humid forest of the Maremma, is considered a true living monument for its centuries-old oaks, maples and elm trees.

Due to its unique characteristics and the beauty of the place, the forest has been declared a real natural oasis to be preserved intact. It has recently been decided to fence off the area, covering about 24 hectares, to ensure adequate protection for a very fragile ecosystem.

The forest is sheltered by a broad stretch of coastal sand dunes, around which grow clumps of lentiscus, myrtle and juniper bushes, where the presence of the sea can always be felt.

In setting up the itinerary according to the project of Mariachiara Pozzana and opening it to the public, the attempt has been made to emphasize the mystery and sacred nature of this place.

Only through art and poetry is it possible to approach such a natural environment without risk of harming it.

In the vicinity of the oak trees most significant for size and shape (the oldest ones have diameters of several meters around the trunk) works in bronze by the sculptor Marcello Guasti have been placed.

Each sculpture is accompanied by the verses of poets (among them Eugenio Montale, Mario Luzi, Dylan Thomas and Dino Campana) placed on fallen tree trunks. In the vicinity of the park is an educational workshop designed to provide school children with an approach to the marvels of nature and the forest, and a 'book tree' dedicated to the oak.

To know more

E-mail:
parchi.valdicornia@parchivaldicornia.it
Web: parchivaldicornia.it

A work in bronze by Marcello Guasti

HOW TO ARRIVE

Between Piombino and Follonica, exiting from S.S. 1 Aurelia.
Address: Loc. Carlappiano, Piombino, Livorno.
tel.: +39 0565 226445, +39 348 8883165
(only for summer period)
fax: + 39 0565 49733
Visiting hours:
By appointment only on weekends in the months of July and August, 3:00 pm – 6:00 pm
Admission: 4,00 €, reduced 3,00 € (under 14, over 65)
Accessible to the disabled - Restrooms

Villa Cetinale

A mingling of sacred and profane

HOW TO ARRIVE

In the vicinity of Sovicille, south of Siena, take the Siena Porta San Marco exit from the Firenze-Siena superstrada (motorway).
Owner: Lord Lambton
Address:
Loc. Cetinale, Sovicille, Siena
tel.: +39 0577 311147
fax: +39 0577 311061
Visiting hours: Monday-Friday, 9:30 am – 12:00 am, by appointment only.
Admission: 6,00 €
Accessible to the disabled - Restrooms

The countryside south of Siena, abounding in sites of rare beauty, arouses emotions that prepare the visitor for Cetinale. Within the park is a splendid formal garden, a number of flower gardens with magnificent roses, peonies, perennials and bulbous plants and above all a splendid Baroque layout with the scope of a landscape sweeping from plain to hillside.

The villa was built by Cardinal Flavio Chigi, a member of the wealthy, powerful family of Sienese bankers who had moved to Rome at the service of the Pope. The building initiative, which lasted from 1676 to 1716, was commis-

Above
The villa

Left
The side garden

150

sioned of the architect Carlo Fontana, a pupil of Bernini, who had already worked on other projects for the Chigi family (in Rome and San Quirico d'Orcia). The building having been rapidly completed, Cardinal Chigi occupied himself with the exterior layout, which was probably also commissioned of Fontana. The architect designed a great axis that starts on the plain with the statue of *Hercules*, traverses the villa with its surrounding gardens and arrives as far as the hillside to conclude in a *romitorio*. An itinerary through the sacred and the profane is rendered even more complex by the presence of a 'thebaide' in the surrounding oak woods.

The woods of the 'thebaide' (the name alludes to the desert in Upper Egypt to which, in the 3rd century AD, many Christian hermits fled to lead an ascetic life) grows around a long network of paths and avenues, with statues of saints and hermits thought to be the work of the sculptor Giuseppe Mazzuoli.

The woods also holds one of the seven votive chapels dedicated to the sorrows of the Virgin, arranged in a sort of circle embracing Ceti-

Romitorio

Thebaide

Holy Stairway

Side garden

Cypress avenue

Villa

First formal garden

Entrance

Entrance to the
cypress avenue

Above, at right
Two views of the side
gardens

Next page
The cypress avenue

nale. It is said that the consecrated *boschetto* was desired by Cardinal Chigi as a place dedicated to
the expiation of a particular sin
of his, having to do with the death
of a rival in love. For some years
in the late 17th and early 18th centuries the famous horserace known
as the Palio of Siena was run in
these woods. It may be that the figures hewn in stone and scattered
through the underbrush, such as
the *Tortoise* and the *Snail* (attributed by some to Mazzuoli), allude
expressly to the Palio.

On the hill facing the villa is the
romitorio. A long avenue now partially lined by cypresses starts from
the villa and runs through a monumental terra-cotta portal decorated by busts and statues in classical style. It then continues up to
a vast open space at the foot of the
hill. We now find ourselves in a theatrical space where the designer
has staged a religious scene; it is
obvious that the *romitorio* serves
the function of theatrical backdrop.
On the facade of the building, several stories high, is a great cross.

The *romitorio* is reached by climbing a steep stairway of nearly 200 steps, immersed in the green woods that surrounds it. Up until the last few years of the 19th century this place was inhabited by 12 hermit friars who visited the chapel in the woods once a month.

Itinerary of visit

From the gate on the southern side of the property appears in the distance, at the end of a long tree-lined avenue, the statue of *Hercules*. Through this gate we enter the **formal garden** with hedges of box and topiaries, embellished by potted citruses and seasonal flowers. The back of the villa and the chapel face on the garden.

On the left a group of gardens flowers in splendor, a real paradise for garden lovers. From beyond the villa the composition can be observed as a whole.

A broad avenue of cypresses slopes gently upward to the small buildings that mark the entrance. Here the avenue narrows to continue, now treeless, for about two hundred meters to the open area at the foot of the Holy Stairway. From here there is a steep climb up the steps to the *romitorio*, from which we can admire the garden, the villa and a landscape still miraculously preserved. From the *romitorio* we descend along the path on the right to the '**thebaide**', where numerous paths running through it, marked with statues, invite the visitor. From here we return to the exit.

To know more

O. Guaita, *Le ville della Toscana*, Rome 1997.

S. Bajard, *Villas et jardins de Toscane*, Paris 1992.

H. Acton, *Tuscan Villa*, London 1973.

E-mail: cetinale@libero.it

Chronology

15th c. Cetinale is owned by the rich and powerful Chigi family, Sienese bankers who then move to Rome at the service of the Pope.

1676 The work of transforming the farm of Cetinale into a manorial residence begins with the building of the villa.

1676-1678 The formal garden and the annexes to the villa are built.

After 1680 Numerous sculptures, probably inspired by subjects of classical culture, are placed around the villa, along the avenue and in the piazzale. Many of the sculptures, the work of Giuseppe Mazzuoli, have now been lost or moved elsewhere.

1687 The colossal statue of *Hercules* is finished.

1698-1705 The great oak woods stretching to the east of the villa is transformed into the 'thebaide'.

1716 The *romitorio* is built.

1977 The Chigi family sell Cetinale to Lord Anthony Lambton.

Villa di Vicobello

A masterpiece by Baldassarre Peruzzi

HOW TO ARRIVE

In the city.
Owner: Selina Bonelli
Zondadari
Address: Viale Bianchi
Bandinelli 14, Siena
tel.: +39 0577 248574
fax: +39 0577 332460
www.vicobello.it
For information and
reservations:
margherita@vicobello.it
Always open in the
weekends only.
Visiting hours:
9:00 am – 12:00 am;
3:00 pm – 7:00 pm
Admission: 10,00 €
(reduced only for
groups). Guided visits
also without appoint-
ment.
Partially accessible to
the disabled
Restrooms

The garden of fruit
trees

Next page
The lemon garden

Both villa and garden were built by the Chigi family in the 16th century. The project is generally attributed to Baldassarre Peruzzi, the architect of many villas and gardens in the territory of Siena. The building, which exists in close symbiosis with the surrounding garden, is undoubtedly one of the masterpieces of villa architecture in the Sienese territory. In 1770 Giacomo Casanova stayed here, as guest of Violante Chigi, who became a close friend of the writer and philosopher at the death of her husband. According to the scheme customary in Tuscany, the garden was terraced in front of the building. The 16th century design conferred perfect spatial organization on the villa, inserting it at the center of a courtyard which was bounded on the back by the the service annexes and the *limonaia*, on the southeast by the lemon garden

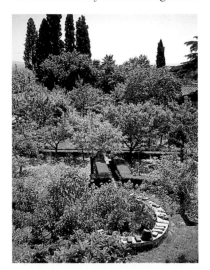

and on the northwest by the *boschetto* of ilexes.

The heraldic emblem of the Chigi family, the mountain, recurs in the great boxwood topiaries from modern times and appears again in the forecourt of the villa and on the third terrace.

The spatial scheme is organized along two main axes, one at right angles to the villa, the other parallel to it, cutting the lemon garden in half. To this simple, austere plan was added, in the 19th century, a third garden below the second terrace, which now houses the orchid greenhouse. In the forecourt of the villa stands the chapel, a building of very elegant lines.

Itinerary of visit

From the courtyard behind the villa we enter the **lemon garden** through an elegant terra-cotta portal. The garden is bounded by walls lined with hedges of evergreen and on the northern side, the *limonaia* where citrus trees were sheltered in winter. It is divided into four compartments, each in turn divided into four sectors with a circular element at the center. Based on the perfect symmetry, balance and the rationality of the parts, it may be presumed that the garden's design dates from the 16th century. This refined geometry is emphasized by the hedges of box that border the lawns dotted with lemon urns. At the back of the eastern wall and along the entrance axis a terra-cotta **exedra** closes off the garden, enhancing the intimate, enclosed effect. The exedra attributable for the simple elegance of its design to Baldassarre Peruzzi is composed of an ample niche surmounted by a molded pediment bearing at its center the Chigi coat of arms. Within it is a circular stone bench and a table.

A ramp of stairs connects the lemon garden to the orchard, where fruit trees were probably grown originally (according to the Tuscan tradition in which the terrace below the house was usually designated as *pomario*, or orchard). Divided into three sections, each in turn subdivided into four beds bordered in box, it is embellished by the splendid flowering of antique roses of 19th century taste. Below the ancient fruit garden a narrow terrace with an orchid greenhouse called the 'botanical garden' concludes the eastern side of the garden.

The last terrace is that of the **belvedere**, reached by descending a double ramp of stairs. This part of the garden ends in an unusual fishpond in the shape of a half moon.

The chapel beside the villa

155

Castello di Celsa

"Tornati a Celsa, e guarda
Che la quiete mia non ti sia tolta"

HOW TO ARRIVE

In the vicinity of
Sovicille, south of
Siena, take the Siena
Porta San Marco exit
from the Firenze-Siena
superstrada (motorway).
Owner: Livia Aldobran-
dini Pediconi
Address: Celsa, Sovi-
cille, Siena
tel.: + 39 06 6861138
fax: +39 06 68195912
Visiting hours: only
upon presentation of
request in writing and
for groups of at least
4 persons.
Restrooms

Situated on the crest of a hill overlooking the Rosia valley, the castle takes its name from the Sienese family Celsi who built it in

unrefined / come back to Celsa and watch / that my peace is never stolen from you).

In the ancient woods and the garden with its adjacent hunting park, silence is still today the fundamental element.

The only sounds to be heard are those of wind, water and birds. This absence of sound becomes music, melding with the broad expanse of the great terraced lawns, cultivat-

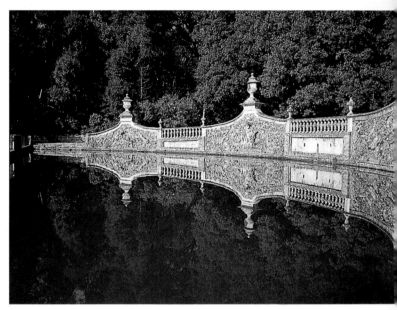

The fishpond

near the end of the 13th century. In the 16th century it was transformed into a villa, probably by Mino Celsi, a man of letters and member of the Sienese *Accademia degli Intronati*, who owned it together with his uncle Cristofano. Celsi recalls the shady peace of the estate at the beginning of his translation of Horace's second Ode, in a dedication to the Archbishop of Siena Francesco Bandini Piccolomini. "Tu canzonetta mia rozza/ed incolta", sang the Sienese poet and humanist, "tornati a Celsa, e guarda/che la quiete mia non ti sia tolta" (You my little song /rough and

ed in the past, that follow each other in succession to merge into the surrounding landscape. In the distance appears a view of Siena, perfect and reassuring as in a 15th century painting.

The name of the castle is linked to the work of Baldassarre Peruzzi (1481-1537), the architect of numerous Sienese villas and gardens. He was responsible for the circular chapel built of brick, elegant in style, and probably also for the terraced wall parallel to the entrance avenue and the **terraced garden** sloping down the hill toward the valley, with its travertine stone vas-

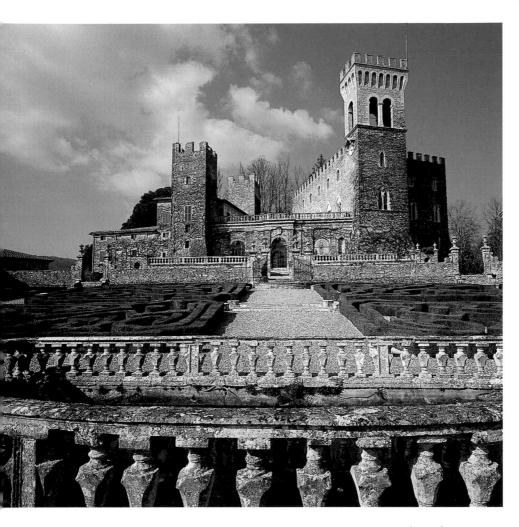

es and potted citrus trees. With these transformations, in keeping with the Renaissance concept of villa, the Medieval castle found itself inserted in a logic of perspective and symmetry. The new wing formed an inner courtyard closed off by a wall with three elegant portals opening onto the surrounding landscape (a solution similar to the one adopted in the castle of Belcaro).

The gardens of Celsa, transformed during the Baroque period, consist today of the 16th century terraced garden and the side garden with its fine hedge of cypresses, great fishpond and parapet decorated in relief patterns.

In the late 19th and early 20th century Maria Antinori Aldobrandini decided to renovate the castle in neo-Gothic style, commissioning the architect Mariani to carry out this project.

Luminous mullioned windows in the facade as well as imitation crenellations and battlements were added. Presumably during the same period numerous tall trees, mainly cedars and ornamental conifers, were planted. Today these trees stand out on the great lawn in front of the fishpond.

The castle seen from the garden

In the postwar years Luisa Aldobrandini, mother of the present owner, made another change.
The garden in front of the building was embellished by box beds planted in the shape of the Aldo-

The avenue leading to the fishpond

with fine statues, fountains in the wall and a semicircular pool. At the sides stand two buildings; the one on the left used as *limonaia* is lit up in spring by the flowering of 'Alba Plena' Banksian roses.

At right
A cypress topiary

brandini coat of arms, composed of stars and rakes, and the cypress hedge that links the garden to the fishpond at the edge of the hunting park was added.

Itinerary of visit
The imposing castle dominates the terraced plain stretching before it. The entrance avenue, flanked by rural buildings, some of which are used today for country tourism, leads directly to the castle. A splendid **tier** of terra-cotta and travertine steps radiating outward leads to the first level and then to the courtyard. From there we descend to the enclosed garden, adorned

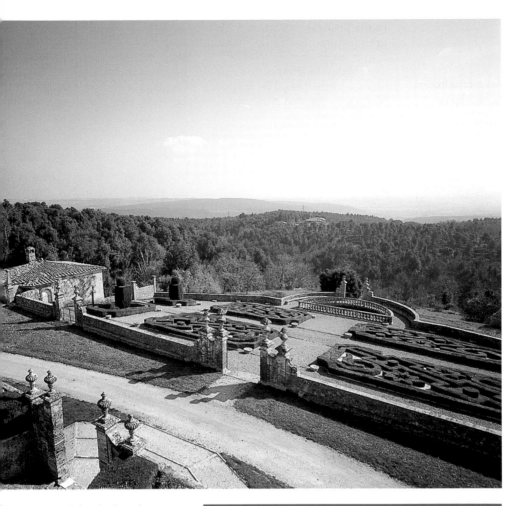

The garden with box beds and
the semicircular pool

Stone, water and evergreens

*"The Italian garden does not exist for its flowers; its flowers exist
for it: they are a late and infrequent adjunct to its beauties, a par-
enthetical grace counting only as one more touch in the general
effect of enchantment. This is no doubt partly explained by the difficulty of cultivating any but spring flowers in so hot and dry a climate, and the result has been a wonderful development of the more
permanent effects to be obtained from the three other factors in gar-
den-composition – marble, water and perennial verdure – and the
achievement, by their skilful blending, of a charm independent of
the seasons.*
*It is hard to explain to the modern garden-lover, whose whole con-
ception of the charm of gardens is formed of successive pictures of
flower-loveliness, how this effect of enchantment can be produced
by anything so dull and monotonous as a mere combination of
clipped green and stone-work".*

Edith Wharton, *Italian Villas and their Gardens*, New York 1904.

Returning to the castle we continue eastward along the avenue
flanked by clipped hedges of
cypress. Through well-kept lawns
the path leads to the splendid **fishpond**. Of semicircular shape, it has
a wall decorated with river gods,
marine animals and travertine
urns. From here a system of
straight paths radiates out through
the great park of ilexes, once used
for hunting.

159

Geggiano

A theater in a garden

HOW TO ARRIVE

In the vicinity of
Geggiano, along
S.S. 408.
Owner: The Boscu
Bianchi Bandinelli family
Address: Via di Geg-
giano 1, Pianella, Siena
tel.: + 39 0577 356879
fax: + 39 0577 357075
For information and
reservations:
villadigeggiano@tin.it
Visiting hours: by
appointment only.
Guided visits for groups
of at least 8 persons
Luncheons, dinners,
wine and olive oil tast-
ing (own production)
organized upon request.
Olive oil and wine sold.
Bookshop

This page
The orchard

Next page
The theater

At right
The villa seen from
the orchard

The estate of Geggiano, crown-
ing a low hill, is reached
through a long *cerchiata* of ancient
ilexes. The villa was created by
reconstructing an older building.
In the 1760s, when Domenico
Bianchi Bandinelli married his second wife Cecilia Chigi Zondadari,
it is probable that a modest manor
house with tower was transformed
into a beautiful country residence
(the tower can still be seen at the
center of the building).
On the occasion of this work, the
fine garden still admired today was
also created. The part of the garden in front of the villa, familiar-
ly known as the *piazzone*, on the
same axis as the building, is closed
off at the back by an interesting
'garden theater'. It is reached by
a central path that, running
between parterres of box, connects
the building to the garden architecture.
An axis at right angles to the one
that links the villa to the little theater leads to the *selvatico* on one
side and to the orchard/garden on
the other, distinguished by an elegant semicircular **fishpond**.
An encircling wall decorated with
terra-cotta sculptures surrounds
the entire orchard and garden,
opening to the outside through six
monumental gates, they too decorated with terra-cotta sculptures.
The 'garden theater' is a typical
feature of the 17th century Baroque
garden. Created at a relatively late
date, Geggiano's garden theater is

nonetheless the finest element in the entire composition.

We know for certain that it was constructed before 1783, the year in which Vittorio Alfieri recited one of his tragedies there (the chamber in which the poet slept, furnished with the opulent bed with baldachin of the times, can still be seen. The cultural interests of the Bianchi Bandinelli family are clear; in addition to inviting such a famous poet as Alfieri, they also called upon foreign artists to work in the villa).

In front of the garden theater stage stand two brick buildings bearing

the coats of arms of the Bianchi Bandinelli and Chigi Zondadari families on the coping.

Niches in these buildings hold statues of *Comedy* and *Tragedy*. A tall cypress tree heightens the perspective effect, making the stage seem deeper than it really is.

To know more

L. Bonelli Conenna, E. Pacini, *Vita in villa nel Senese*, Ospedaletto/Pisa 2000.

Web: www.uehha.org/it/Toscana/geggiano.htm

Chronology

Before 1530 The Geggiano estate, a simple country residence probably surrounded by an orchard/garden, belongs to the De Santi family

1530 Geggiano, brought as dowry, becomes one of the possessions of the noble Sienese family Bianchi Bandinelli.

c. 1768 The country residence is transformed into a true villa and is furnished with an interesting garden centering around the 'garden theater'.

End of 18th c. The villa is splendidly frescoed by the Tyrolean painter Ignazio Molder, who in the long gallery on the ground floor, depicts various aspects of country life, the cycles of nature and scenes inspired by the Commedia dell'Arte. In this work Molder draws inspiration from the drawings of Giuseppe Zocchi and the engravings of Francesco Bartolozzi. The pictorial program is further enriched by portraits of famous personages of the times: from the lord and lady of the house Anton Domenico and Cecilia to the famous singer and musician Perellino, shown with his actress daughters. Nature and theater are linked in a single representation.

1824 Ownership passes from Giulio Ranuccio Bianchi Bandinelli, first Napoleonic prefect of the Department of the Ombrone and then Governor of Siena, to his eldest son Mario, who makes no great changes. From Mario, through various hereditary transitions, it comes down to its present owners.

L'Apparita

The Sienese landscape becomes a garden

HOW TO ARRIVE

In the vicinity of Ginestreto, along S.S. 223.
Owner: Don Giovanni Guiso
Address: Strada Ginestreto 1, Siena
tel.: +39 0577 394241
fax: + 39 0577 394241
Visiting hours: by appointment only
Partially accessible to the disabled
Restrooms

The theater

This page
One of the inscriptions in the garden

At right
The entrance to the villa

Situated to the south of Siena, in a dominating, panoramic position, the fine brick building with its splendid side loggia is traditionally attributed to Baldassarre Peruzzi.
Although certain documentation is lacking the villa, so elegant and harmonious, truly seems to indicate the hand of a master. It is not really a villa but a manor house, that is a fine, comfortable dwelling place but not one so elegant as to be surrounded by a sumptuous garden. Before 1966 the garden did not exist; only the Sienese countryside extended all around the building.

can landscape, transforming them into a garden.
This conceptual procedure has led to the invention of what can be called a garden/landscape, an absolute, emblematic place where the Tuscan landscape is reproduced in synthesis, and where Porcinai may have reached his highest peak of creativity.
Although today the initiative seems minimalist, so natural and harmonious is the result, Porcinai has in reality wrought profound changes.

The garden was created by Pietro Porcinai for the present owner, who was prepared to understand and strongly support the proposals of the great landscape artist, undoubtedly highly innovative.
The garden of the Apparita is one of Porcinai's most original creations. It reiterates, in fact, the salient characteristics of the Tus-

The transformations brought about by the architect can be clearly evaluated only by examining aerial photographs taken before, in which the agricultural nature of the area is clear.
By large-scale earth movement the landscape artist reinterpreted the entire system of access roads, now moved lower and further away

from the house. The avenue rises with great naturalness through olive groves flanked by clumps of Scotch broom, which seem to have existed forever but have instead been artfully planted.

We then arrive at the quadrangular parking lot, lowered so that it is invisible from the house, partially covered by roofing. From here a gently sloping path leads up to the house between two steep banks covered with lavender to form a sort of plant gallery.

The front door, rendered monumental by an original arch of ivy, opens in the simple brick facade of the building.

From here the path becomes circular, running around the house to the garden theater. Composed of simple benches and surrounded by hedges of broom, the essential structure of the theater recalls, for its situation, Greek theaters, which always faced on a panorama so beautiful as to evoke a sense of the divine. Few but fine terracotta ornaments and some inscriptions are the elements by which the eye is caught before sweeping over the landscape in the direction of Siena.

The Apparita garden is essential and evocative as only a perfect Sienese landscape can be. Gentle rolling hills modulate a horizon rhythmically broken by the vertical soaring of cypresses against the sky.

The Tuscan landscape takes on the appearance of an ideogram, calling to mind a page of Japanese signs.

Framed by two cypresses, Siena appears in the distance, like a Renaissance model of the ideal city, its profile barely softened by the summer haze.

The benches
in the theater

163

Horti Leonini

Eternal springtime

HOW TO ARRIVE

Along S.S. 2 Cassia headed toward Rome.
Address:
Piazza della Libertà, San Quirico d'Orcia
tel.: +39 0577 897211
Visiting hours:
from 8:00 am to sunset; possible visits in the evening in summer only.
Free admission
Guided visits by appointment.

Around 1560, Grand Duke Cosimo I granted to Diomede Leoni ownership of the area, situated under the towns wall of San Quirico d'Orcia.

The construction of the garden went on for years and in 1581 it was not yet complete, although

creator, and the lion appears in fact on the two heads placed on the entrance portal.

Originally there were four entrances, the main one on the city square, the one in the back near the Church of Santa Maria ad Hortos, the one situated halfway down the northern wall, marked by two pilasters, and the little door above, opened in the wall.

Through a vestibule paved in brick and enclosed by walls and clipped ilexes, we enter a *parterre* in the shape of an elongated rhombus.

The *parterre* near the town walls

Leoni had, it seems, already spent large amounts in renovating the town wall standing along one side of the garden.

The owner was authorized to build a path on top of the wall so that both the garden and the valley of the Orcia could be admired from above.

The garden was called *Horti Leonini* from the name of its owner and

The design of the *parterre* is highly original: a star-shaped pattern of triangular beds visually enlarges the space available, which is animated still further by the different heights of the box hedges around the beds.

At the center stands a statue of Cosimo III, sculpted in 1688 by Giuseppe Mazzuoli and coming from Palazzo Chigi in San Quirico. Through a ramp cut out of the *selvatico* of ilex trees the central avenue leads to the upper level, where a great lawn stretches as far as the town walls.

On this lawn, bounded by a majestic 'crown' of ilexes, once stood the imposing Medieval tower, destroyed by German troops in 1944. From here another ramp leads down to an avenue of ilexes trimmed to form a wall of vegetation, and then to the **rose garden** (recently restructured) that bounds the lower part of the garden.

("neither far away nor for long"), clearly expressing the love of its former owner for his garden and his wish never to leave this place for long.

The garden is filled with inscriptions recalling themes dear to Diomede, as demonstration of the profound meaning it must have held for the man who created it and lived in it: *"omitte mirari beatae / fumum et opes strepitumq. Romae"* (Be no longer fascinated by the frenetic activity of happy Rome"); *"peregrino labore fessi /*

The *parterre*

We know that Diomede Leoni had a house in the garden, and that he was granted permission to cut four windows and a little door in the town wall. The house may be identified as the *palazzina* leaning against the wall on the southwest side. Inside it a fireplace bears the inscription *"nec procul nec longe"*

venimus larem ad nostrum" (wearied by the fatigue of wandering we have returned to our hearth"); *"nihil agis / insidias in me componis inanes"* ("be calm. Sooth my futile worries"); *"hic vitabis aestus"* ("here you will find shelter from the torrid heat"); *"hic ver assiduum"* ("here is eternal springtime").

Giardino di Palazzo Piccolomini

A window on the Val d'Orcia

HOW TO ARRIVE

Along S.S. 2 Cassia in the direction of Rome. The palace is in the center of Pienza, about 50 km from Siena.
The garden can be visited only on the occasion of very special events but may be seen from the museum inside the palace.
Tel. museum:
0578 748503

This little garden, whose surface area is about the same area as that of the palazzo, admirably exemplifies the type of walled garden that, in the 15th century, represented the worthy completion of a palace in the city. In the 15th century, an open, panoramic space on an axis with the courtyard was a truly innovative concept. Enea Silvio Piccolomini (who became Pope Pius II in 1457) commissioned Bernardo Rossellino to transform the little town of Corsignano into a modern city, which was given the name Pienza. The work went on from 1459 to 1464, the year when both the client and the architect died. In his *Commentari* Pope Pius II describes the construction of the garden, conceived as a garden and "hanging orchard, suitable for grapevines and other trees". The land was filled in and leveled to have a flat plane in front of the house. Planted to fruit trees, the place was furnished with a stone balustrade and seats "brightened with colored pinnacles that form a gallant spectacle from afar". The garden appears today in the layout given it in 1910, on the occasion of the restoration of the palazzo built by Silvio Piccolomini and carried out on the basis of documentary sources, with the intention of harmoniously reconstructing the original scheme. Divided into four sections bordered by double hedges of box, the garden has a central fountain, rounded topiaries of laurel, gravel paths and beds of flowering roses. It is enclosed by an ivy-covered wall; on the southern side

The garden seen from the palazzo

three windows have been opened in place of the original parapet, presumably damaged during the years of neglect. The simultaneous view of the palace courtyard and the garden, in the blinding light of the Sienese sky, is an unforgettable experience. Looking into the garden through the openings in the wall we remain suspended in a timeless space enveloping the landscape of the Val d'Orcia.

To know more
M. Mangiavacchi, *I giardini del Senese fra '800 e '900; sei esempi a confronto*, in "La memoria, il tempo, la storia nel giardino italiano fra '800 e '900", edited by V. Cazzato, Rome 1999, pp. 286-288.

La Foce

A landscape of giants and demigods

In the extraordinary landscape of the Val d'Orcia, arid and almost barren in summer, slashed by the deep eroded ditches of the *crete*, Villa La Foce and its splendid garden are an unexpected oasis of serene repose. This is undoubtedly one of the most beautiful modern gardens in Tuscany. It is probable that the owner Iris Origo, a refined writer and author of the historical novel "The Merchant of Prato", perceived this place as a landscape marked by striking contrasts. In the late 1920s she and her husband Antonio bought an abandoned estate and transformed it into a magnificent villa with a model farm. The English architect and landscape artist Cecil Pinsent, a friend of Iris Origo, was commissioned to carry out the work, in a project that went on until 1939. He created the great garden in different stages, but always according to a unitary logic, drawing inspiration from the formal gardens of classic Italian tradition. Pinsent

HOW TO ARRIVE

Between Chianciano Terme and Pienza, Chianciano Terme exit from the Firenze-Roma A1 highway.
Owner:
Benedetta Origo
Address: Strada della Vittoria 61, Chianciano Terme, Siena - tel. and fax: +39 0578 69101
For information: info@lafoce.com
Visiting hours: only on wednesday afternoon. Guided visits from October to March at 3:00 pm and 4:00 pm. From April to September at 3:00 pm, 4:00 pm, 5:00 pm and 6:00 pm.
Admission: 10,00 € as contribution to a non profit company (not compulsory)
Partially accessible to the disabled
Restrooms

The geometric garden

"Below me lay the fields beside the river – land potentially fertile, but then fallow, which would be flooded when the rains came by the encroaching river-bed. Against the sky, behind the black rocks of Radicofani, dark clouds were gathering for a storm [...] Suddenly an overwhelming wave of longing came over me for the gentle, trim Florentine landscape of my childhood or for green English fields and big trees – and most of all, for a pretty house and garden to come home to in the evening. I felt the landscape around me to be alien, inhuman – built on a scale fit for demi-gods and giants, but not for us".

Iris Origo, *Images and Shadows*, London, 1970.

also renovated the building and designed the *limonaia* and other annexes.

In 1927 the first formal garden, bounded to the south by a wall with a fountain and a green grotto concealed by a dome of laurel, was built in front of the house. From here a path leads to the lemon garden, begun in 1933. It is adorned by box trimmed in spherical shapes and bordered along the sides by herbaceous plants and splendid peonies. The transverse axis of the garden continues, rising along an avenue of cypress trees to the top of the hill.

In 1939 the monumental **geometric garden** was laid out below the lemon garden. It is reached by

The geometric garden

Cecil Pinsent, the architect of gardens

Cecil Ross Pinsent was one of the most important garden architects in Tuscany in the first half of the 20th century. Born in Uruguay in 1884, he returned with his family to England while still a child. There he studied architecture at the Architectural Association of London. In 1906 he moved to Florence, where he met Bernard Berenson, the famous art historian who was one of his first clients. In 1909 Pinsent worked, in fact, on Villa I Tatti, at Ponte a Mensola near Settignano. The results of this project were brilliant, and numerous others followed, with the architect creating the gardens of Villa Le Balze (1911), Villa Medici (1915), and Villa La Foce (starting in 1927), his longest and most ardently enthusiastic project.

Pinsent's gardens revive the architectural nature of the Italian formal garden, through the use of box hedges and topiaries long with grottoes, fountains and statues that the architect himself designed with great creative talent and craftsmanship, frequently carrying out the material execution as well. Better than any other architect, he knew how to interpret the desires of his clients, for the most part British or Americans members of the highly cultivated, sophisticated colony enamored of Florence and Tuscany.

descending a stairway built of Rapolano travertine. Below the stairway is a grotto. Bordered by great box hedges, dominated by four magnolias and enclosed by high walls of cypresses, the triangular space ends in a pool and a statuary group.

A long **pergola** of wisteria bounds the formal garden at the top, while of cypresses planted by Iris Origo in homage to Florentine 15th century painting.

Continuing up the slope we find an informal garden with aromatic and Mediterranean plants where the geometric structure of the garden gradually drifts off into the woods.

Near the woods is a little family

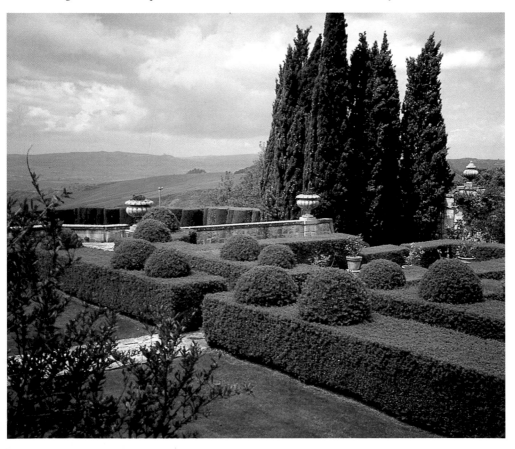

The formal garden

on the other side of the *berceau* runs a narrow terrace containing a rose garden with borders of lavender and herbaceous perennials, among which emerge clumps of *aubretia* and *alyssum*. Following the wisteria pergola we arrive at a strikingly panoramic spot overlooking the broad **landscape** of the Val d'Orcia, marked by the avenue graveyard, where Iris' son, who died at the age of six, is buried. This space too was designed by Pinsent as a garden enclosed by cypresses with tombs placed amid box beds and a chapel in Renaissance style.

To know more
Web: www.lafoce.com

Castello di Brolio

A neo-Medieval garden

HOW TO ARRIVE

Near Castellina in Chianti, Poggibonsi exit from the Firenze-Siena super-strada (motorway).
Owner:
Baron Bettino Ricasoli.
Address: Brolio, Gaiole in Chianti, Siena
tel.: +39 0577 7301
fax: +39 0577 730225
Visiting hours:
9:00 am – 12:00 am,
3:00 pm – 6:00 pm.
Closed on Fridays in winter.
Admission: 3,00 €
Restrooms

The garden in front of the castle

Next page
The garden below the castle bastions

The castle, from time immemorial an outpost of great strategic importance in the wars between Florence and Siena, has been destroyed and rebuilt several times over the course of the centuries. The present aspect of the estate is however due almost entirely to the 19th century initiative of Bettino Ricasoli, the Iron Baron whose name is closely linked to the history of the Italian Risorgimento. Around 1835 Ricasoli decided to rebuild a neo-Gothic castle over the old Medieval ruins. The castle was then completed by the Sienese architect Giuseppe Partini (1842-1895). The vast and complex building was built of brick (typical of Siena, but less common in the Chianti). This makes it quite easy to distinguish the 19th century renovation from the Medieval remains consisting of the ancient encircling wall and the base of the castle keep.

Itinerary of visit
An avenue of cypresses leads up to the castle through the so-called '**English woods**' planted by Bettino and Vincenzo Ricasoli starting in the 1840s. The Ricasolis gave a romantic touch to the park, but focused not so much to the design of the whole as on the selection of the species, in keeping with the fashion of the time for botanical collections. At Brolio rare and exotic species were planted, in particular **conifers** grown from seeds that Bettino and Vincenzo exchanged with other collectors or brought home from their travels: the sequioa (*Sequoia sempervirens*), the Spanish fir (*Abies pinsapo*), the Himalayan cedar (*Cedrus deodara*) and many other species still to be seen today. The park occupies the northern side of the hill (as can be

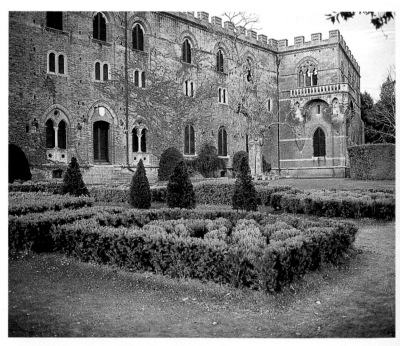

seen from a *cabreo*, or map of the farm dated 1838), arriving to touch on some of the castle buildings.

A small and recent formal garden of simple geometric design lies before the main facade of the castle. Low box hedges border parterres of lavender cotton (*Santolina chamaecyparissus L.*). Nearby stand ancient trees: an ilex (*Quercus ilex L.*) and a great **sterculia** (*Sterculia sp.*), unfortunately damaged by cannon fire in July 1944. From the bastions of the wall, which opens to the south over a marvelous panorama of vineyards and woods sweeping from Monte Amiata to Volterra, can be seen a fine **Italian garden**.

Here in the past was the castle moat, probably a 19th century reinterpretation of formal Renaissance models. The garden follows the curve of the wall with a simple, elegant geometric design of box hedges decorated with potted citruses. A long row of Bengali roses separates it from the surrounding countryside.

At the death of Bettino and Vincenzo the park was cared for first by Elisabetta, Bettino's daughter, and then by his grandson Giovanni, both of them ardently botany enthusiasts. Giovanni was a friend of Giuseppe Gaeta, the creator of the Moncioni park near Montevarchi, and author, in 1899, of the *Catalogo delle specie presenti nel parco di Brolio*.

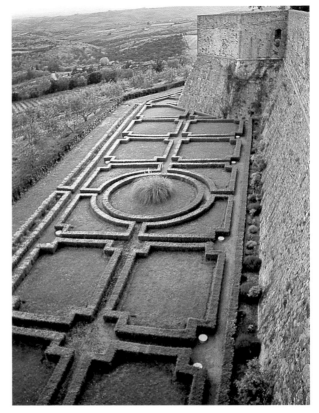

To know more

L. Bosi, *Il Chianti di villa in villa*, Rome 1985.

L. Bosi, *Le ville del Chianti*, Pistoia s.d.

O. Guaita, *Le ville della Toscana*, Rome 1997.

E-mail: Barone@Ricasoli.it

www.ricasoli.it

Chronology

1009 The first information on Brolio dates from this year. Bonifacio, Marchese of Tuscany, grants the property to the monks of the Badia Fiesolana.
1432 The castle of Brolio is forced to surrender to the attacks of the Sienese militia led by Antonio Petrucci, who holds prisoner for some time members of the Ricasoli family, yielding only to the Florentine troops led by Neri Capponi.
1478 The castle is attacked and almost entirely destroyed by Aragonese troops. It is then rebuilt by the Florentines due to its important strategic position in the Sienese territory.
1530 The castle returns to Florentine jurisdiction after having been again destroyed by Siena during the siege of Florence. Under the Grand Duchy grandiose projects are planned for its restoration and enlargement, which then become useless with the peace stipulated between Florence and Siena. Having lost its strictly military function, the castle becomes the manorial residence and farm of the Ricasoli family.
1835 Bettino Ricasoli decides to restore the castle in Gothic style. The project for the park is drawn up by Bettino Ricasoli himself assisted by his brother Vincenzo, an expert botanist.
1843 Grand Duke Leopolo II orders built the new road that joins Gaiole to Castelnuovo Berardenga. The event is celebrated by stone inscriptions placed on this occasion at the beginning of the new access avenue (flanked by cypress trees) at the desire of Bettino Ricasoli.
21st c. The estate belongs to the Ricasoli family. The area of the English woods has only recently been restored.

Badia a Coltibuono

A Medieval orchard

HOW TO ARRIVE

In the immediate vicinity of Gaiole, Valdarno exit toward Montevarchi from the Firenze-Roma A1 highway.
Owner: the Stucchi-Prinetti family
Address: Badia a Coltibuono, Gaiole in Chianti, Siena
tel.: +39 0557 744832
fax: +39 0557 744839
info@coltibuono.com
www.coltibuono.com
Visiting hours:
May – October
(closed August) from Monday through Friday with visits every 30 minutes from 2:30 to 4:30 pm
Admission: 4,00 €
Guided visits

Badia a Coltibuono is situated on a hilltop not far from the important Etruscan archaeological area of Cetamura, where a long ridge marks the boundary between Chianti and Valdarno, on the road that links Gaiole in Chianti to Montevarchi.

Since the Middle Ages Coltibuono has been the vital center of a great agricultural estate that has grown and flourished over the centuries, also through donations to the Vallombrosian Abbey given by landowners in the area.

Still today Coltibuono is surrounded by vast conifer woods planted for the first time by the monks who followed San Giovanni Gualberto.

The most striking aspect of the place is the extraordinary conservation of the surrounding landscape, which forms a background to the buildings and the garden of rare beauty.

The garden, supported by a wall on one of its longer sides, has been replanted in rather recent times and still bears traces of the ancient plots of the Medieval orchard, clearly visible. The vast rectangular space is divided by perpendicular paths into seven sections occupying the lower level of the garden. The paths are partially covered by a rustic **pergola** of grapevines, wisteria and laburnum. At the end, on the edge of the road, stone steps lead down to another small formal garden.

Facing on the largest sector, divided by boxwood hedges, are the windows of the monastery, now a private residence.

At the center is a simple rectangular basin in stone around which winds the complex design of the hedges, bordering beds of roses decorated with topiaries and potted citrus trees. Some of the square

The formal garden

The pergola
and the formal garden

The Badia

sectors are planted to lawn, others to fruit trees.

Among the latter a **Medieval orchard** has been skillfully reinterpreted in a modern key, reiterating the division into plots containing aromatic and medicinal plants, flowering perennials, peonies and raspberries.

To know more

F. Majnoni, *La Badia a Coltibuono-Storia di una proprietà*, Florence 1981.

Chronology

770 The first core of the Badia is mentioned in a document from the Ricasoli archives.

11th c. Coltibuono passes under the control of the Benedictine Abbey of Vallombrosa.

1446 Paolo da Montemigliaio, the new Abbot of Coltibuono, begins to improve the property.

1488 Giovanni de' Medici, the future Pope Leo X, takes possession of the Abbey.

c. 1710 New major projects for the transformation of the building complex.

1810 Subsequent to the Napoleonic edict that determines suppression of the religious corporations, the monks of Coltibuono are forced to leave the Badia. Various owners succeed each other over the years.

21st c. The Badia offers overnight accommodations for guests. Courses in Tuscan cooking are held (in English).

173

Fonterutoli

Marianna's garden

HOW TO ARRIVE

From the Firenze-Siena Superstrada (motorway), exit San Donato, take the way to Castellina for about 5 km toward Siena, Loc. Fonterutoli.
Owner: the Mazzei family
Address: Loc. Fonterutoli, Castellina in Chianti, Siena
tel.: +39 0577 73571
fax: +39 0577 735757
For information: www.fonterutoli.com
fonterutoli@fonterutoli.it
Visits by appointment only

The ancient village in which stands the Villa of Fonterutoli, not far from Castellina in Chianti, was once an Etruscan-Roman settlement, as confirmed by its Latin place name (*Fons Rutilans* or *Fons Rutilii*) and the Etruscan tombs found in the vicinity. Fonterutoli played a major role in the history of the Florence-Siena relationship since it was here, in the early 13th century, that diplomats from the two cities met to try to reach an agreement on the border between their lands.

Particularly interesting are the ancient farm, which has belonged to the Mazzei family since 1435, and the villa, dating from a slightly later time, which has undergone some changes over the course of the centuries (for example, the loggia overlooking the formal garden was added in the early 20th century).

The villa, sober and elegant in appearance, is surrounded by three different gardens: the formal garden, of neo-Medieval style; the **rose garden**; and the *boschetto* of romantic taste. The three gardens are located in an elongated area that starts in front of the villa.

The formal garden, in the shape of an irregular square, is a typical Italian garden with regular sectors bordered by hedges of box.

Probably of late 19th century design, it was restored in the 1930s. From here the visitor, seated under a *berceau* formed of two ancient *Sophora japonica*, can enjoy the splendid panorama of the Sienese Chianti hills.

The villa seen from the garden

Next page, at left
The rose garden

At right
The formal garden

The garden is bounded on one side by a high stone wall, shielded by imposing ilexes; the other side opens onto the rose garden.

The rose garden was created at the same time that the formal garden was restored at the wish of the owner of the time, Marianna Mazzei Tommasi Aliotti.

The elongated area is divided into beds of curious shape, planted with clumps of roses and decorated with great citrus urns.

The interesting perspective effect

is heightened by a stone arch that forms a backdrop to the entire composition.

High hedges of evergreens (box, viburnum, laurel) separate the modern part of the garden from the little **romantic *boschetto***. Narrow, winding paths run through the *boschetto*, shaded by ancient ilexes, as well as plane trees and horse chestnuts planted more recently (*Platanus x acerifolia, Aesculus hippocastanum*) and thickets of bamboo (*Phyllostachis nigra*). In the nearby wine cellars an excellent Chianti classico (*Castello di Fonterutoli*) is still produced, as it was centuries ago.

In one of the little shops in the village perfume and other products coming from the fields of lavender are sold.

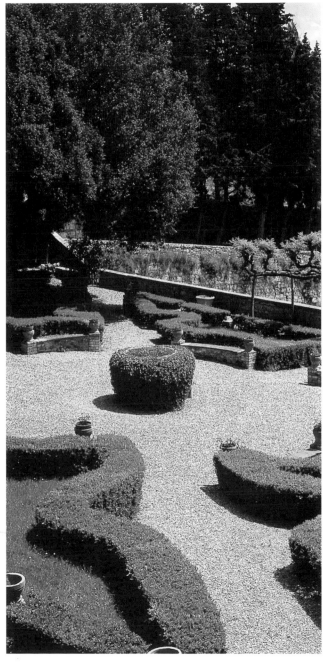

To know more
O. Guaita, *Le ville della Toscana*, Rome 1997, pp. 378-380.
I giardini del Chianti, edited by G. Romby, R. Stopani, Florence 1989, p. 109.

Giardino Passerini

Farm and garden

HOW TO ARRIVE

Between Cortona and
Pergo, Arezzo or
Valdichiana exit from
the Firenze-Roma A1
highway.
Privately owned.
Address:
La Chiesa 2-4, Pergo,
Arezzo.
The garden is not easy
to visit. For information
call the Garden Club
of Florence,
tel.: +39 055 282245

The great plane tree

The entrance
to the garden

The Villa of Pergo, lying in the green basin of the Val d'Esse, is surrounded by a beautiful garden dating from the 17th-18th century. The villa is distinguished by its elegant architecture. It was built in the 17th century by the Mancini family (in the chapel is an inscription from 1632 dedicated to Simone Mancini). Later it became the property of the Passerini family, who still own it today.

The layout of the Pergo estate is one of the best examples of that ensemble of rational initiatives carried out by the enlightened landowners of Cortona which, during the course of the 18th century, transformed the Val d'Esse into a great garden.

Pergo appears today, in fact, like an extraordinary agricultural park, structured with great beauty and functionality through broad tree-lined avenues, cultivated fields, walls dividing the orchards, an ornamental garden and beyond it a long *ragnaia*. Through the regular organization of avenues and paths, the countryside enters the garden and blends with it harmoniously.

The gate opens onto a wide avenue where, on the right, stands in all its majestic beauty an ancient **plane tree** (*Platanus orientalis*),

declared garden monument and protected by the law on Italy's historical and artistic heritage.

Continuing along the avenue of linden trees in the direction of the villa, we find on the right the large **basin/pool** constructed in 1733. In the shape of a trapezoid, it has a rectangular artificial island in the center, linked to the mainland by a double-arched masonry bridge. On the island grow two *Albizzia julibrissin*, silk trees bearing pink flowers.

Beyond the pool, to the right and the left, are two walled gardens, once orchards. Across meadows shaded by tall trees and conifers we go on to arrive at the villa. The building, with its fine interior decorations, is a typical example of villa architecture in the Cortona area. From the western side of the villa we enter the lovely **formal garden** divided into four beds bordered in box with *Magnolia x soulangeana* trees, a central fountain and a neoclassical *tempietto*. The garden ends at a very unusual building called the *poledraia*, which may once have been used as a stable (it

The Val d'Esse

The ensemble of villas, gardens and cultivated fields that meets the eye of the visitor traversing the Val d'Esse forms a very particular landscape that calls to mind 18th century theories on the *ferme ornée*, or, in a literal translation of the French term, the 'decorative farm'. A *ferme ornée* is an estate made up of farmland, meadows and vineyards, and managed according to principles of utility. Economic and productive requisites are, however, usually brought into harmonious accord with the particular beauty of the places. "Anything that is pretentious, that tends toward the noble, the grand, the majestic, cannot properly appear here". This principle is especially appropriate to the Val d'Esse and its particular features, such as the simple beauty of its villas and the sobriety of the scenery. In 1833 Emanuele Repetti was struck by the landscape with "the perspective of a varied, most pleasant countryside, irrigated by copious perennial springs, sprinkled with country houses and lordly villas amidst numerous rows of vines and olives, not far from forests and boundless fields of grain and artificial prairies".

The pool with its island

is now a lemon-house). The interior, with cross-vaulted ceiling, is decorated with curious scenes of military life from the Napoleonic era. Behind the villa, in the deepest shade, is a lovely **camellia garden** sheltered by a *Magnolia grandiflora* and enclosed by walls decorated in *trompe l'oeil*.

Near the northwest boundary of the estate can still be seen the great *ragnaia* of evergreens used in the 18th century for bird-catching.

To know more

M. Pozzana, *I giardini di Cortona*, in "Bollettino Ingegneri", May 1996, n° 5, pp. 3-8.

Villa Sandrelli

The peasant and his wife in the garden

HOW TO ARRIVE

The Valdichiana exit from the Firenze-Roma A1 highway.
Owner:
Alberto Sandrelli and Maria Sofia Sandrelli Duranti
Address:
Via Lauretana 1, Camucia, Arezzo
tel.: +39 0575 603128
Visiting hours: by appointment only
Accessible to the disabled.

Built in the first half of the 18th century by a descendent of Marsilio Tommasi, the villa is situated in the center of Camucia; at the time it was built it was almost the only house in the village.

The pretty **garden**, covering about half a hectare, was created from 1753 to 1764 (the work was amply documented in a notebook of accounts kept by the owners), while the villa was completed in 1749 and the two side wings in

In 1928, at the time when the estate passed into the hands of the Sandrelli family, the 18th century *pomario* was also transformed, becoming an ornamental garden with hedges and clipped spheres of box (the tuje were planted at an even more recent time).

Lying on a gentle slope, the small garden of the villa is laid out in two parts, the one nearest to the house composed of the flower garden and *pomario*; the other, lower down and linked by a stairway, occupied by a *ragnaia* and the orchard. Originally the two areas clearly coincided with the different uses of the garden itself: one more closely linked to villa life and to 'enjoyment', the other to agriculture and utility.

The formal garden

1777. Beside the main body of the villa are a little *limonaia* and the farm.

The garden, although changed over the course of time, still clearly shows today its original 18th century structure.

Enclosed by a wall decorated with terra-cotta vases and sculptures, the part nearest the villa was transformed in the late 19th century by the addition of informal flower beds and tall trees.

On the wall enclosing the lower part of the garden are two **wall-fountains** with calcareous decorations now unfortunately ruined. In the two niches stand the figures of the *Villanella*, or peasant woman, holding a basket of fruit, and the *Villano*, or peasant, in popular costumes, both typical personages of 18th century garden decoration. The niche with the *Villano* has been changed by the addition of a clock.

Parco Tommasi Aliotti

A miniature Villa Marlia

Ferdinando Chiostri, in his book on Tuscan parks, compares this villa to that of Marlia for the breadth and scope of its natural scenery. He is struck by the fascination of the place, the *genius loci* that confers on the estate a beauty and majesty enhanced still further by the lovely pond lying before it. "Beautiful is the basin in front of the villa", notes Chiostri, "an embellishment certainly not very ancient, but one which notably contributes to the beauty of this place".

The villa, an elegant three-storey building with a very simple facade bounded to the east by a fine chapel and to the west by a *limonaia* of exotic style, owes its fascination both to its position and to the transformations carried out during the course of the 19th century, on the basis of the existing 18th century structure. Niccolò Tommasi created the present villa by radically renovating, in the second half of the 18th century, a property that already existed in the 16th century. The accounts listing his expenses include, in 1774, costs for "having rebuilt half of the house to be used as villa, a chapel, and half of the peasant's house, about one thousand six hundred *scudi* at least".

In the following century Luigi Tommasi (1827-1903) transformed the estate into an English garden, planting a fine collection of trees and adding numerous decorative features. Still today, amid examples of *Sequoiadendron giganteum*, *Abies pinsapo* and *Cupressus fune-*bris, we find stone benches, rock gardens and a *romitorio*.

To the sides of the entrance avenue, now lined with cypresses, vast farmlands stretch out within the park. The avenue leads to the pond, then divides to run along two great flower beds where **pink peonies** explode in blossom.

Behind the villa is an imposing *cerchiata* of ancient ilexes. A lovely path meanders through the great park around it.

HOW TO ARRIVE

In the vicinity of Camucia, Valdichiana exit from the Firenze-Roma A1 highway.
Owner: the Tommasi Aliotti family
Address: Case Sparse 639, Loc. Metelliano, Cortona, Arezzo
tel.: +39 0575 603394
Guided visits upon request
Accessible to the disabled - Restrooms not for disabled

The corridor of ilexes behind the villa

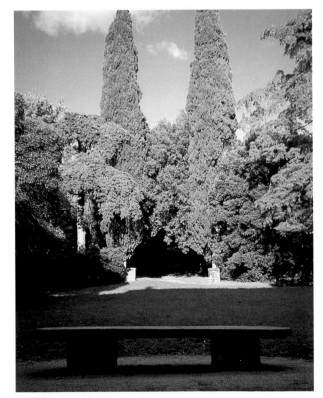

179

Villa Guillichini

Warriors in the garden

HOW TO ARRIVE

Not far from Arezzo, Montevarchi exit from the Firenze-Roma A1 highway.
Privately owned.
Address: Tregozzano, Arezzo
Visiting hours: the garden, now undergoing restoration, cannot be visited easily
Accessible to the disabled
tel.: +39 055 570216
(Università internazionale dell'Arte, Centro studi sul giardino e il paessaggio)

Villa Guillichini, located at Tregozzano near Arezzo, is surrounded by one of the most important gardens in the area.

Near the end of the 16th century the building belonged to Francesco di Agnolo Guillichini. It was described as an "estate of lands cultivated to vineyards, orchards and a portion to olive and mulberry trees, with the manor house". In the first half of the 17th century the villa belonged to Lodovico di Francesco Guillichini, juryconsult and professor of civil institutions at Pisa as well as Knight of Santo Stefano. Lodovico had the chapel of Santo Stefano built, adjacent to the villa but for public use, already around the middle of the century. In 1730 Rosa Guillichini Berardi sold the estate to her sons. At the death of the two ecclesiastics, the property was inherited by their nephew Angiolo (1736-1814).

It was Angiolo who first enlarged the villa by encapsulating at the back the most ancient part and extending the left side of the building by adding to it a short wing. In the 19th century the villa, owned first by Giovan Francesco and then by his son Luigi, underwent further renovation, particularly on the occasion of the wedding of Luigi and Marianna Albergotti.

Dating from 1831 is the layout of the park with its *parterre* and the formal garden below, once adorned with statues. The construction of the right wing used as *limonaia*, of the theater and the planting of the surrounding woods date instead from 1873. In 1880, on the occasion of the sale by Giovan Battista to his brothers, the villa, the *boschetto*, the *ragnaia* and the citrus trees were assessed. Also listed was "the portion of lawn that lies before the two buildings... a portion of land kept as vineyard where there exist several low Grapevines and various Fruit Trees, some benches, three terra-cotta Statues, a Column with an eagle, and various pilasters encrusted with glass and marble, plus a Room for keeping Flower vases". Many of these elements no longer exist today.

Created in the course of the 19th century, the garden and park ensemble stretches over a sloping hillside. The formal garden contains beds bordered in box with a pool at the center; located in front of the house, it is enclosed by a wall and preceded by unusual towers serving as guard post (it is easy to imagine two armed warriors rushing out of the towers to defend the garden). Majestic trees stand in the English garden, distinguished by an outdoor **theatrical space** with a fine 19th century construction serving as backdrop.

The geometric
parterre

Giardino di Venzano

A nursery of aromatic herbs

This is the garden of an interesting nursery. The two owners, Australians, have designed it with refined British taste, placing a fine selection of herbaceous and aromatic plants around an ancient building, a former Augustinian monastery. An ancient row of pomegranates and old jujuges bear witness to the previous arrangement of the area around the residence, which has only recently been transformed into a succession of **secret gardens** enclosed by hedges of laurel. On the walls of the house today flower roses of the Kiftsgate and Cooper's Burmese varieties.

The idea of creating the nursery-garden was suggested to the owners by the presence of a spring and of the ancient monastery. The abundance of water facilitated nursery production, while the monastery evoked recollections of the *'giardini dei Semplici'*, of medicinal and aromatic herbs, used in the past for curative purposes and in monastery cuisine. The nursery specializes in aromatic plants and perfumed flowers, medicinal plants, antique roses and classic carnations, flowers beloved by the 15th century. But it also grows quite rare exotic species, offering collectors examples not to be found elsewhere in Tuscany. The choice of herbaceous plants is extremely varied, oriented toward species that can withstand the local climate and are best suited to well-drained land and dry summer weather – rosemary, lavender, cysts, thyme, and perfumed pelargoniums. Lavender cotton, *teucrium fruticans*, lavender and thyme blend

pleasantly with the green landscape of the rolling Sienese hills, forming silvery clumps along the dry-stone walls.

One of the owners of the garden-nursery is a painter who specializes in pictures of flowers, reproduced with the 'dotting' technique used in the 17th century by Giovanna Garzoni.

To know more

E-mail: venzano@sirt.pisa.it
Web: www.florealia.com/venzano.asp

HOW TO ARRIVE

Take the Via Volterrana to Volterra, then toward Colle Val d'Elsa, until the road-fork for Mazzola.
Owner: Donald Leevers
Address: Loc. Mazzola, Venzano, Pisa
tel. and fax: +39 0588 39095
Visiting hours:
Thursday – Sunday, from March to December 15,
10:00 am – 1:00 pm,
3:00 pm – 6:00 pm
Guided visits by reservation
Partially accessible to the disabled
Restrooms

Above and below Aromatic and perennials herbs in the garden

Other gardens in Tuscany

Castello di Belcaro
Loc. Belcaro, Siena
The garden is now undergoing restoration and visits will not be possible in brief periods.
tel.: + 39 0577 394237
A lovely forest of ancient ilexes surrounds the castle rebuilt in 1525, perhaps by Baldassarre Peruzzi. Within the wall lies the lemon garden with urns scattered over the lawn.

Castello di Cafaggiolo
Barberino di Mugello
Visiting hours: by appointment only for groups
tel.: +39 055 8479396
The Medicean castle, rebuilt in the early 15th century by Michelozzo di Bartolomeo, conserves only the plan of the Renaissance garden, totally transformed in the 19th century. Today it contains tall trees, ancient mulberries and a sequoia.

The theater
of Villa Bernardini

Castello di Montegufoni
Via di Montegufoni 20, Montagnana
Val di Pesa, Florence - tel.: +39 0571 671131
Privately owned. Visits are not allowed
The garden, not large in size, consists of hedges of cypress and box planted by the English Sitwell family, owners of the magnificent castle for three generations. The 18th century grotto inspired by the myth of Galatea with automata once moved by hydraulic mechanisms is highly interesting. The castle is used today for country tourism.

Certosa di Pontignano
State Road 408 in the direction of Pianella, Loc. Pontignano, Castelnuovo Berardenga, Siena - Visiting hours: 8:00 am – 2:00 pm weekdays only. Visits are possible for groups and schools only and by reservation via fax.
Free admission
tel.: +39 0577 356851
fax: +39 0577 356669
The monastery, founded in 1343, was sold in 1784 to the hermits of Monte Celso and then to the Sergardi family. Today it is owned by the University of Siena, which organizes conferences and seminars there. The garden retains some of its original features, such as the rectangular fishpond and the *ragnaia* of clipped ilexes for bird-catching on the northern side. Fine collection of potted lemon trees.

Le Corti
San Casciano, Florence
Visits are possible only on the occasion of special events - tel.: +39 055 820123
A monumental avenue of cypresses leads to the beautiful villa. The garden consists of a broad lawn around the house, a *boschetto* behind it and a terrace with flower beds. In the month of September the garden is open for the 'Giardini in Fiera' exhibition.

Orto Botanico di Lucca
Via del Giardino Botanico 14, Lucca
Visiting hours: from Monday to Friday 9:30 am – 12:30 pm; weekends 11:00 am – 5:00 pm.
tel.: + 39 0583 442160
fax: + 39 0583 442161
Founded in 1820 by Maria Luisa di Borbone, the garden has an arboretum, a hillock and a pond, as well as a botanical school and greenhouses. Important collections of medicinal plants, rhododendrons, camellias and spontaneous botanical species used in the Lucchese cuisine.

Orto Botanico di Pisa

Via Luca Ghini 5, Pisa
Closed Sundays and holidays. Free admission. tel.: +39 050 2215350
fax: + 30 050 551345
Closed for restorations from July 1, 2002, to April 30, 2004

Luca Ghini founded the Orto in 1544, when Cosimo I summoned him to take the chair of botany at the University of Pisa. This is Europe's oldest botanical garden. In 1591 the Orto was moved to its present location, between Via Santa Maria and Via Roma, by Giuseppe Casabona. In 1752 the facade of the gallery was transformed by the addition of decorations in *pietra spugna* and calcareous concretions typical of 16th century grottoes. In the Orto grow centuries-old trees: a *Magnolia grandiflora* and a *Ginkgo biloba* planted in 1787, a *Platanus occidentalis* from 1808, a myrtle planted in 1815 and a camphor tree (*Cinnamomum camphora*) introduced around 1842. Of extraordinary historical and scientific importance are the naturalist collections and the herbarium of dried plants (*Herbarium Horti Pisani*).

Roseto Botanico Carla Fineschi

Locality Casalone, Cavriglia, Arezzo
Visiting hours: from dawn to sunset
tel.: + 39 055 966638
fax: + 39 055 9124331
The most important collection of roses in Italy, created by the owner Gianfranco Fineschi in decades of ardent collecting, containing thousands of species and varieties.

Torre Guinigi

Via Sant'Andrea (Palazzo Guinigi), Lucca
Visiting hours: all days from Nov. 1 to Feb. 28, 9:00 am – 5:30 pm; from March 1 to Sept. 30, 9:00 am – 9:00 pm; from Oct. 1 to Oct. 31, 10:00 am – 6:00 pm
Admission: 3,10 €, reduced 2,70 €
tel.: 39 0583 316846
A garden or rather a *boschetto* of ilexes planted on the terrace of a tower that dominates the whole city. The garden was used by members of the family as a delightful place of repose.

Villa Bernardini

Via di Vicopelago 573/A, Vicopelago, Lucca
Visiting hours: from Apr. 1 to Oct. 31, 9:30 am – 12:00 pm / 3:00 pm to 7:30 pm. From Nov. 1 to March 31, 10:00 am – 12:00 pm

The garden of the Certosa di Pontignano

/ 2:30 pm – 5:30 pm. Visits by appointment only - tel. and fax: + 39 0583 370327
A fine late Renaissance villa completed in 1615 by the Bernardini family (as indicated by the inscription over the front doorway). The villa is surrounded by a large park with *limonaia* and a fine garden theater in box clipped in spherical shapes, dating from the mid-18th century.

Villa Borrini

Pieve di Compito, Lucca
tel.: + 39 0583 977066, at lunch and dinner time; visits by appointment only
This lovely 19th century villa, usually not open to the public, is surrounded by a stupendous garden of camellias. In the immediate vicinity of the villa, at Sant'Andrea di Compito, is the nursery of Guido Cattolica, a descendent of the Borrini family. Ancient camellia trees grow here, as well as the original species and varieties of the villa garden.

Villa Gori Muratori Ginanneschi

Strada di Ventena 8/10 - Siena
Visiting hours: by appointment only
tel.: + 39 0577 44305/44705
Important 'garden theater' with stage paved in pebble mosaic. The theater is linked to the villa by an ancient avenue of ilexes. A second ilex avenue leads to the 'garden maze'.

Villa di Gricigliano

Via di Gricigliano, Loc. Gricigliano, Pontassieve, Florence
tel.: +39 055 8360254/5 (Municipality of Pontassieve, Cultural Bureau)
Usually not open to the public, the imposing villa, dating from the 16th century, is

surrounded by a broad moat filled with water. The great exedra-shaped lawn was once a *cavallerizza*, an area used for horse racing. Other interesting features are a terraced garden with wall-fountain, an elegant nymphaeum and a loggia; to the north is a great *selvatico* of ilex trees. The villa, once the property of the Martelli family, is now owned by the religious order of the Sacro Cuore di Gesù Redentore. In the nearby 18th century chapel, it is possible to participate in the sung mass and Gregorian chant.

Villa di Gricigliano

Villa I Busini
Castiglioni di Rufina,
Loc. Scopeti 28, Florence
Visiting hours: by appointment only on Fridays
tel.: + 39 055 8397809
The villa originated in the 15th century; enlarged over the years, in the early 20th century it was embellished by a fine formal garden built over an existing system of terraces. The villa is now used for country tourism.

Villa di Meleto
Via Meleto 25, Castelnuovo d'Elsa, Castelfiorentino, Florence
Visiting hours: by appointment only
tel.: +39 055 570216 (Università internazionale dell'arte, Centro studi sul giardino e il paesaggio).
An Italian garden with fine box beds created at the turn of the century over 18th century terraces. In the 19th century Cosimo Ridolfi introduced new systems of experimental agriculture.

Villa Puccini
Via Dalmazia, Pistoia
Visiting hours:
always open
Free admission
tel.: +39 0573 21331 (public relations office of the city hall of Pistoia)
The great park, today divided into several estates, was created by Luigi de Cambray Digny and in part by the City of Pistoia, which has opened it to the public. The romantic pond with tempietto is especially interesting.

Villa Roncioni
Strada Sotto Monte in the vicinity of San Giuliano Terme, Pisa.
Visiting hours: by appointment only
tel.: +39 050 818047
An interesting park created in the first half of the 19th century by Alessandro della Gherardesca, who also designed the neo-Gothic building where silk worms were raised.

Villa Rucellai
Via di Canneto 16, Prato
Visiting hours: by appointment for groups maximum 10 persons - tel.: + 39 0574 460392
This beautiful villa, now used as a hotel, grew up around a Medieval tower. It has a fine terraced formal garden with boxwood topiaries, offering a magnificent view over the valley of the Bisenzio.

Flower shows and exhibitions

Borgo a Mozzano (Lucca)
Azalea show (*April*).

Florence
Giardino dell'Iris
Iris show (*April-May*).

Giardino dell'Orticoltura
Important flower show (*end of April*).
Tuscan nurseries participate.

Palazzo Budini Gattai
Camellia show (*end of March*).

Lucca
Villa Oliva
Exhibition of topiary art (*June*).

Along the walls of the city
Murabilia (*september*).
Nurseries from all over Italy participate.

Pescia (Pistoia)
Biennale flower show (*September*).
Dedicated to cut flowers.

Pieve di Compito (Lucca)
Camellia show (biennale) (*March*).

San Casciano (Florence)
Villa Le Corti
'Giardini in Fiera' (*September*).
Nurseries from all over Italy participate.

Glossary

Aviary A great cage often in the form of a pavilion where exotic birds are kept.

Balustrade Balustrades usually consist of small shaped columns forming parapets.

Baroque garden A 17th-18th century garden which interprets in a particularly theatrical manner the perspectives of the 16th century garden.

Bowling green A lawn of rectangular shape used in English gardens for bowling (or other outdoor games)

Boschetto A small grove of trees.

Cabreo list of holdings or property illustrated by detailed maps

Casino di delizia An urban pavilion around which lies an ample garden having both agricultural and ornamental features. Widespread in Tuscany in the 17th century.

English garden An informal landscape garden which became popular all over Europe in the 19th century.

Fabrique French term for the little constructions widely used in 18th century parks: *tempietti*, grottoes, pavilions and so on.

Fagianeria A fenced-in area with annexed construction where pheasants were raised.

Flower garden An enclosed, protected area in which flowers are grown. For Renaissance gardens the term secret garden is also used (see).

Formal garden (see *Italian garden*).

French garden A garden created according to the rules of perspective and decoration developed in France in the 17th century. It is distinguished by avenues bordered by elaborate *parterres de broderie* (see) and *boschetti* clipped in shapes.

Gabinetto di roccaglia Italian for *cabinet de rocaille*, a restricted space adorned by rock gardens.

Gamberaia A pool for crayfish raised for the kitchen. A place name recurrently found in Tuscany derives from the name of the pool.

Garenna (or rabbit island) An artificial island in the center of a pool or pond where rabbits were kept during the Baroque period.

Garden of acclimatization Garden of scientific nature in which exotic plants are grown to study their adaptability to a different climate.

Garden room (see *stanza di verzura*).

Giardino dei Semplici Garden of medicinal herbs. From the Medieval Latin *medicamentum simplex*: "medicine made with herbs".

Grotto Garden architecture designed to imitate natural caves. Very frequently used starting from the early 16th century. It often has a vaulted ceiling decorated with *pietre spugne* and other materials (see *polimaterico*).

Italian garden A geometric garden of limited size. Widespread in Europe in the early 20th century, in coincidence with the revival of the Renaissance Italian garden (see also *formal garden*).

Jardin potager The French term for orchard or vegetable garden.

Lawn Broad grassy area often located in front of the villa; heightens the effect of the building.

Limonaia (or *stanzone* for citrus trees) A rectangular building where citrus trees are sheltered in cold weather. A lemon garden is often found in front of the *limonaia*.

Mascaron Human or animal head, often deformed in grotesque style, used from Renaissance times on for the decoration of fountains.

Nymphaeum Grotto inspired by Roman nymphaeums, places sacred to water nymphs.

Parterre Group of flower beds. The etymology of the term is uncertain; it either derives from the Latin *partiri*, to divide into sections, or from the French *par terre*, "on the ground". *Parterre de broderie* is the French term used to indicate beds of particularly elegant design, recalling lacework; used in the classic French garden from the 17th century on.

Polimaterico Type of decoration used in Renaissance and Baroque grottoes, formed of various materials: marble, *pietre spugne*, shells, ceramic elements and so on.

Ragnaia A little wood of clipped evergreens where nets were stretched to catch birds.

Romitorio A building often in the form of a ruin designed to call to mind a hermit's dwelling place.

Rustic decoration Decoration made of rough-hewn stones or *pietre spugne* taken from natural caves.

Secret garden An enclosed, protected area where flowers are grown. For Renaissance gardens the term flower garden is also used (see).

Selvatico (or *salvatico*, archaic) A *boschetto* of evergreen trees, often ilexes, contrasting with the ornamental garden with its flowers, beds and hedges.

Spugna (or *pietra spugna*) Calcareous concretions coming from natural caves; used to decorate grottoes.

Stanza di verzura or **Garden room** A part of the garden bounded by hedges or rows of trees. From this term derives the expression *'giardino a stanze'* or *'a camere'*, that is composed of various garden rooms.

Teatro di verzura or **Garden theater** A garden room (see) designed like a theater.

Topiary The art of clipping trees and shrubs in geometric ornamental shapes.

Verzura Archaic term indicating vegetation.

Analytical index

Index of gardens